THE
AMAZEMENT
REVOLUTION

Praise for *The Amazement Revolution*

"Practical, tactical and hands on, this book will push you to initiate the customer interactions you should have been doing all along."

—**SETH GODIN**, author
Poke the Box

"In reading Shep Hyken's *The Amazement Revolution*, I applaud his approach. At American Express we view service not as a cost, but an investment in building customer relationships. Through Relationship Care—our overarching service ethos—we strive to emotionally connect with our customers and add value to every interaction. The seven strategies outlined in this book are exactly how we operate."

—**JAMES P. BUSH**, Executive Vice President,
World Service, American Express

"The true measure of Shep Hyken's success as a communicator is simple. His books always exceed the readers' expectations. *The Amazement Revolution* is no exception!"

—**J. KIM TUCCI**, Co-Founder,
The Pasta House Co.

"*The Amazement Revolution* will serve as a guide for many business operators as they pursue paths towards developing and communicating an effective mission, as well as establishing the strong culture needed for success. The book is a demonstration of the importance of attaining effective team leadership."

—**J RONALD E. HARRISON**, Retired SVP, PepsiCo, Inc.,
Currently member of the Board of Managers, RE/MAX, LLC

"We have a retail store that competes with other stores who sell exactly what we sell. Why do our customers do business with us? It's not because of our prices. It's because of our service. We give our customers a better experience. *The Amazement Revolution* reveals many of the secrets that give us a competitive advantage over our competition."

—**KEITH BAIZER**, Mayor of Creativity,
Artmart, Inc.

More Praise for *The Amazement Revolution*

"Our family has been in the roofing business since 1929. How have we been successful for so many years? All you have to do is read the first chapter of this book to know. We just do the right thing."

–**BOB FREDERIC**, President,
Frederic Roofing

"In *The Amazement Revolution*, Shep not only inspires but provides a clear path for moving from a service culture to an Amazement culture and backs it up with real world examples. Whether a sole practitioner or a corporate giant ,if you desire to create Amazed customers you need to read this book!"

–**BARRY G. KNIGHT**, President
NEXT Financial Group, Inc.

"What is your trademark? Why do your customers want to return? My good friend Shep Hyken is a mirror image of successful repeated business. After all, this is his ninth book! This Cowboy knows his stuff."

–**JEFFREY W. HAYZLETT**, best-selling author of
The Mirror Test, Celebrity CMO, Cowboy

"It takes more than just great technology for our customers to think of us as more than "just another software vendor." The chapter on cultivating partnerships is exactly what we do to create value and build customer loyalty."

–**RON CAMERON**, President
KnowledgeLake
Honored as Microsoft Partner of the Year

BOOKS BY SHEP HYKEN

Moments of Magic: Be a Star with Your Customers and Keep Them Forever

The Loyal Customer: A Lesson from a Cab Driver

Only the Best on Success (co-author)

Only the Best on Customer Service (co-author)

Only the Best on Leadership (co-author)

The Winning Spirit (co-author)

Inspiring Others to Win (co-author)

The Cult of the Customer: Create an Amazing Experience that Turns Satisfied Customers into Customer Evangelists

The Amazement Revolution: Seven Customer Service Strategies to Create Amazing Customer (and Employee) Experiences

For information about the above books contact:

Shepard Presentations, LLC
(314) 692-2200
info@hyken.com
www.hyken.com

THE
AMAZEMENT
REVOLUTION

Seven Customer Service Strategies to Create
an Amazing Customer (and Employee) Experience

SHEP HYKEN

GREENLEAF
BOOK GROUP PRESS

658.8
HYK

For ordering information or special discounts for bulk purchases, please contact Shepard Presentations, LLC at 314.692.2200 or info@AmazmentRevolution.com.

Published by Greenleaf Book Group Press
Austin, Texas
www.gbgpress.com

Distributed by Greenleaf Book Group LLC
PO Box 91869, Austin, TX 78709, 512.891.6100

Cover design by Greenleaf Book Group LLC
Interior design and composition by Jerry Dorris, AuthorSupport.com
Content editing by Brandon Toropov
Line editing and proofreading by Lauren Manoy, Ambitious Enterprises
Indexing by Carol Roberts

Publisher's Cataloging-In-Publication Data
(Prepared by The Donohue Group, Inc.)

Hyken, Shep.
    The amazement revolution : seven customer service strategies to create an amazing customer (and employee) experience / Shep Hyken. -- 1st ed.
    p. ; cm.
    Includes index.
    ISBN: 978-1-60832-106-3
    1. Customer services. 2. Customer relations. 3. Communication in organizations. 4. Interpersonal relations. I. Title.
HF5415.5 .H956 2011
658.8/12   2011920528

Part of the Tree Neutral® program, which offsets the number of trees consumed in the production and printing of this book by taking proactive steps, such as planting trees in direct proportion to the number of trees used: www.treeneutral.com.

Printed in the United States of America on acid-free paper
11 12 13 14 15 10 9 8 7 6 5 4 3 2 1
First Edition

TreeNeutral

TABLE OF CONTENTS

PART ONE: *What Is Amazement?*

PART TWO: *The Master Class*

PART THREE: *Role Models for Amazement*

PART FOUR: *Create Your Own Amazement Revolution*

AUTHOR'S NOTE: When I use the word "customer" in this book, please understand that I mean the whole range of people who do business with, and rely on, your organization. This could be someone you are presently calling a customer, client, patient, guest, member, etc. As we go through the book, you will see the phrase "customer" used most frequently to describe the members of this group. This is just a "catch all" term to describe someone you do business with. Whatever the label, I'm always talking about the same group of people.

PART ONE

WHAT IS AMAZEMENT?

amazement (noun) 1. overwhelming surprise or astonishment. —*Webster's Unabridged Dictionary.*

Amazement (proper noun) Service that is consistently and predictably better than average. Amazement is not necessarily about "Wow!" levels of service, although sometimes it may be. It is about an all-of-the-time, I-know-I-can-count-on-it, better-than-average experience. Most organizations can be better than average some of the time. Very few, however, are consistently better than average. That consistent experience is what sets apart an average organization from one that is Amazing! —Shep Hyken

CHAPTER ONE

THE RIGHT THING TO DO

From the time I could write, whenever I got a present, my mom would say, "Write a thank-you note. That's what you do when you receive a nice gift."

That simple-sounding instruction was really about a whole lot more than writing a note. It was part of my parents' larger philosophy about what was right and what was wrong in life. There were certain things you did, and certain things you didn't do, in your relationships with others.

Although this wasn't a customer service principle, it was a life lesson, and it was a lesson that eventually had profound implications for me, my business, and for a whole lot of people who read my book *The Cult of the Customer*. What I eventually came to call the Amazement Revolution—the strategic decision to remake your organization or your team based on the principle of amazement—was actually rooted in my parents' philosophy. The Amazement Revolution is all about doing what's right by the important people in your life.

I believe that if you do what's right, then things like customer service and marketing and sales have a way of looking after themselves. If you don't, they become very difficult.

This book is about the seven specific strategies that amazing service organizations consistently do right when it comes to relationships with their customers and their employees. These seven strategies also serve as declarations of principle for the organization as a whole. If you build these seven Amazement Strategies into your organization, lots of important things—like writing thank-you notes—become second nature.

I think we all know what doing the right thing for customers feels like when we experience it in our own lives *as* customers. It's much harder to identify the principles and processes that make "doing the right thing" on a consistent basis possible for an organization, but I know it can be done. Let me give you an example from my own childhood.

I'd been practicing magic—card tricks, rope tricks, and so on—since I was about ten years old; around the age of twelve, I experienced something totally unexpected. A brave mother asked me to perform a magic show at her son's birthday party. I remember getting paid $15 for that forty-five-minute show, which was a pretty big deal.

Suddenly I was a professional magician! At dinner one night, after that first show for my first paying customer, my mom said, "Don't forget to write a thank-you note." Other "command performances" followed. These were birthday party magic shows, and every one I did resulted in a payment from a grateful parent. I always worked hard on my routines, and I made sure at the very end that I "magically" produced enough candy for the kids, so that even if the show had left something to be desired, the audience would still love me.

I did as my mom said—and more important than that, I followed the *spirit* of what she'd said. I wanted to do right by the families who had invited me to entertain at their parties. Following my mother's lead, by the ripe old age of twelve I had learned to develop some "do the right thing" processes for my little business:

- A week before the booking for a birthday party or magic show, I called the parent to confirm the time I would be showing up and to get any last minute details.
- I showed up early. This, my dad told me, was even better than being on time.
- I did the best job I could possibly do.
- I made sure I left a little late. I gave people more than they expected.
- I sent a thank-you note the very next day.
- A week later, I would call to make sure everyone loved the show and to say thank you once more. (By the way, these conversations sometimes lead to booking another party.)

When I look at those six steps, I realize just how important they were—and are! My business today operates using precisely the same processes: show up early, stay late, do your best, always say thank you, give people more than they expect, and follow up. There are many other processes now, of course, but these are still in place for me. And they all arose out of this core desire to do the right thing.

I didn't go to school to learn how to execute those processes. I didn't go to customer service training seminars to learn how to talk to people who wanted to work with me. I didn't go to a marketing class to learn how to write the thank-you notes. And I didn't go to a sales training class to close the additional bookings that arose when I made that follow-up call. My parents taught me those skills and reinforced the core principles, which all came down to the single core principle of doing the right thing. Everything else followed from that. The activities may have looked simple, but executing them properly every single time took discipline.

It's the same with the strategies and principles in this book. They are not simplistic, but they aren't rocket science either. They are easily understood, but they take time to get right. What matters is not just that you under-stand them, but that you *integrate* them into your overall business strategy and your overall life strategy—into what you and your team do every day.

The Amazement Revolution is about indoctrinating yourself and your team in the phenomenon known as amazement. The book is built on my own observations, based on over twenty-five years of research and working with clients, about the seven core strategies that an organization of any size can use to instill and reinforce the desire to do the right thing by both customers *and* employees. And yes, those two groups are linked. The first are your external customers; the second are your internal customers. External customers, of course, are the people who pay money for your products, services, or solutions; internal customers are the people who work for your organization.

To keep external customers happy, you must make sure your employees know that you care about doing what's right by them, day after day after day. Your employees will in turn care about doing what's right by the customer. There are lots of lessons and processes in the pages that follow, but they all proceed from the first principle of doing the right thing by your internal and external customers. You have to care about that first. Amaze your employees, and they'll spread the amazement!

After we do the right thing, we can classify what we have done as customer service or marketing or sales or employee relations or whatever. In the moment, though, as my parents would surely agree, *it's just what you should do.* And if you do it consistently, you amaze people.

If you believe, as I do, that it makes sense to do the right thing by both internal and external customers more often; if you want to build a world-class service organization, starting at the bottom, the middle, the top, or at any part of the enterprise, regardless of your current title or level of experience; or if you are simply curious about what this Amazement Revolution is all about—read on!

CHAPTER TWO

HOW WE GOT HERE

This book could almost be considered a sequel to my earlier book, *The Cult of the Customer: Create an Amazing Customer Experience that Turns Satisfied Customers into Customer Evangelists*. I say "almost" because you don't have to have read a word of that book to put the principles of this book into practice. However, you will want to read what follows in this chapter, whether or not you're familiar with the first book. (If you've already read *The Cult of the Customer*, please consider this chapter a brief but essential refresher.)[1]

CRITICAL POINT #1:
YOUR ORGANIZATION HAS A CULTURE

Every organization has an operating culture. Right now, your organization's operating culture either focuses on creating an amazing experience for both internal and external customers…or it doesn't.

Accepting this much is the essential starting point. Whether your organization is large or small, whether you are the founder of the company or a front-line employee, whether you work with customers on the front lines or somewhere deep within the enterprise, *your organization has a culture that determines the quality of the experience you provide* for employees and customers. Your organization's culture falls into one of the following categories:

1. It is *at* the level of amazement, and people are striving to stay at that level.
2. It is *moving toward* the level of amazement, and people are eager to reach that level.
3. It is *stagnant*, and people are, as a group, indifferent about whether or not the level of amazement is ever reached (or they are uncertain about what amazement is).

Look at my definition of amazement again. It's important.

As it applies to customer service, it is a consistently and predictably better-than-average customer experience.

Most organizations' service cultures are not at this level; they're stagnant. Their people are complacent about the level of service they are delivering. As a result, these organizations are moving further and further away from amazement every day.

THE FIVE CULTS

There are five specific cultures—or "cults," as I call them—that I use to more specifically describe an organization's current direction. As you read the list below, ask yourself which one of these cults best describes your organization right now.

The Cult of Uncertainty

- In the cult of uncertainty, either no brand promise has been communicated or the brand promise is regarded as meaningless. As far as the external customer is concerned, there's no consistency to the customer experience. This lack of consistency leads to uncertainty. Sometimes customers have a positive experience with you, and sometimes they don't. Because of this uncertainty, customers might have a poor expectation based on a negative or inconsistent past experience with your organization. At best, these customers simply *hope* for a positive experience. At worst, their "default setting" is a negative expectation. Most customers get used to companies operating in this cult, which is not to say they like it.

- The same dynamic applies to the internal customer (employee) experience. Because the team members haven't been trained properly—or at all—they don't know how to effectively interact with customers, and they don't have the tools they need to do the job well. Job satisfaction is typically low. They have no internal mantra that aligns them with the organization's mission.

An internal mantra is a one-sentence-or-less summary of the service philosophy that aligns employees with the company's mission. This is important because it serves as a constant reminder to employees. An example is Southwest Airlines's internal slogan (mantra), which is: "Not just a career, a cause."

- In the very best-case scenario, the employee *hopes* for a good experience. Again, at worst, their "default setting" is a negative expectation.
- Note: The cult of uncertainty is by far the largest of the five cults. Most organizations operate in this cult. That doesn't necessarily mean they're bad organizations. Instead, a company operating in the cult of uncertainty has a great opportunity to experience its own Amazement Revolution and just hasn't yet taken the steps to do so.

The Cult of Alignment

- In this cult, your organization makes a powerful, emotionally compelling, yet simple brand promise. External customers understand the promise, but they are still waiting to experience it. They want proof.

A brand promise is a concise commitment to customers about what they can expect as a result of doing business with your organization. An example of a brand promise is FedEx's slogan, "When it absolutely, positively, has to be there overnight."

- Internal customers also "get" the brand promise. They have an internal mantra, a one-sentence-or-less summary that that aligns them with the company's mission. They have been properly trained and given good tools, but most do not yet consistently deliver above-average service. Job satisfaction is improving.
- Some brand promises can also serve as mantras and be the same for both internal and external customers. For example, one of my favorite mantras comes from the Ritz-Carlton Hotel chain: "We are ladies and gentlemen serving ladies and gentlemen." It's short, simple, and impossible to forget—and both customers (guests) and employees understand exactly what it means.

The Cult of Experience

- In this cult, external customers experience a powerful, positive *interaction* with your organization that supports a brand promise they understand and remember. They like it and hope that the experience will be just as good as the next time. Confidence is building.
- Employees also experience the mantra/brand promise working, and they begin to look forward to delivering on it. Job satisfaction is on an upward trajectory.

- Note: The transition between the cult of alignment and the cult of experience is usually the most important cultural shift for a specific employee, for a specific customer, and for a customer-focused organization as a whole.

The Cult of Ownership

- Over time, customers experience *multiple* positive interactions with your organization. A positive outcome becomes predictable, and the customer begins to own the experience. The customer thinks, "This is where I want to do business!"
- Employees have a similar experience inside the company as positive interactions become consistent and predictable; employees begin to own the process that delivers good customer experiences. They also begin to implement and refine the processes that deliver multiple powerful, positive interactions with customers. They begin to enjoy significant job satisfaction. They think, "This is where I want to work!"
- Note: Ownership has three requirements. First, internal processes (operational procedures and policies) must be in place that are understood and used by employees. Second, these internal processes must consistently deliver positive experiences to customers. Third, these internal processes must regularly be improved upon. In my experience, no organization can move forward to the cult of amazement, the most desirable cult, unless it meets *all three* of these criteria!

The Cult of Amazement

- Customers get *addicted* to the level of experience they consistently receive, and they become *evangelists* on behalf of your organization. They self-identify as part of your community, and they want others to become part of your community, too. (Evidence of this takes the form of loyalty and referrals.) Mistakes certainly aren't impossible, but when you've achieved the level of amazement, if your organization makes a mistake, the external customer's "default" assumption is that it will be resolved in a positive way. You get a second chance. The bottom line: people trust you and love doing business with you.

- Your employees also connect as a community. They have a shared system of belief, one that elevates the customer experience to primary importance. Employees become evangelists for you as an employer, and they can even aid in the recruiting process. People enjoy their career with you and love telling others about what they do for a living.

Remember: Amazement is not a single experience. It is the *consistent outcome* **of expecting and getting the right thing.**

The cult of amazement involves both customers and employees. Expecting your employees to deliver a superior experience to your organization's customers when they have not enjoyed this unique culture as a result of working for you is worse than unrealistic. It's delusional!

CRITICAL POINT #2:
YOUR ORGANIZATIONAL VOCABULARY MUST CHANGE

The way we communicate *always* affects our behavior. If your organization is currently operating in the cult of uncertainty, not only must your processes change, but your vocabulary must change as well. *When we change our vocabulary, we can change our thinking.*

Each organization has its own needs on this score, and it's likely that no two organizations are going to share precisely the same terminology as they move out of the cult of uncertainty and away from organizational and personal stagnation. The following phrases should become part of the vocabulary of every group, large or small, if you and your organization are committed to moving toward the cult of amazement.

Amazement: You know this one already. It's an experience that is consistently and predictably above average. Amazement is the state of having people do the right thing for us so consistently that we come to expect that treatment; we overlook occasional problems because we anticipate a positive resolution; and we actively recruit others, so they can have the same positive experience we are having.

Amazement Revolution: This is your organization's movement out of anything that resembles the cult of uncertainty and toward the cult of amazement, or your effort to stay in the cult of amazement. This movement must be led by someone. To learn who, see *force of one*, *force of many*, and *force within*, below.

Evangelist: This describes your highest-level customer, the customer who does business with you at the cult of amazement level. This customer is not just loyal, they also sing your praises to others. This customer wants to convert others, turn them into customers, and thus do your marketing for you! Loyal employees do much the same thing by recruiting prospective employees from their circle of friends and family when your enterprise operates within the cult of amazement.

Force of one: This is someone who aspires to achieve or to continue operating within the cult of amazement as a solo entrepreneur.

Force within: This is a person or group within an organization that aspires to achieve or to continue operating within the cult of amazement, even though the enterprise as a whole may not share that objective.

Force of many: This describes the situation where *everyone* in the organization aspires to achieve or to continue operating within the cult of amazement. It's part of the culture. However, the Amazement Revolution is not over. It's an ongoing phenomenon, and the drive to maintain amazement is driven by a leader (typically a CEO, owner, founder, or president) who is focused on people—both employees and customers.

Interaction: This is the phrase with which I propose we replace the common word "transaction." A transaction is something that starts and ends. An "interaction," however, is part of an ongoing relationship. I've made a promise to remove "transaction" from my service vocabulary, and I hope you will do the same in your organization.

Moment of Magic: This is my take on Jan Carlzon's moments of truth concept: "Anytime a customer comes into contact with any aspect of a business, however remote, that customer has the opportunity to form an impression."[2] These touch points can be good, bad, or average, and they can be experienced by both internal and external customers. Positive moments of truth are what I call Moments of Magic. Even though I use the word "magic," that doesn't mean the touch points are always "wow" experiences. Just as we saw in the definition of amazement, these may simply be above-average person-to-person interactions. There's an old saying that a journey of a thousand miles begins with a single step. The journey toward amazement begins with a Moment of Magic!

Moment of Misery: This is the phrase I use to describe negative moments of truth, such as a manager criticizing an employee in public during a team meeting, or an employee failing to assume accountability for a problem reported by a customer. Note: Any moment of truth, even a Moment of Misery, can be transformed into a Moment of Magic! (And vice versa!)

Role model: This is a person or organization engaged in an Amazement Revolution—someone from whom you can learn specific lessons that help you to lead your own Amazement Revolution. I've included more than fifty role models in this book. See Amazement Revolution takeaway below.

Touch points: See Moment of Magic.

Amazement Revolution Takeaway (ART): This is a best practice that you learn from another person or organization and adopt to support your own Amazement Revolution. It's the answer to the questions: "So what? Now what?" Amazement Revolution Takeaways follow every amazement story in this book and are highlighted with the phrase **ART.**

ART of Amazement To-Do List: This is a summary of the specific best practices that you are focusing on implementing within your team or organization. You'll find this list in Appendix A; use it to create your own unique to-do lists.

Amazement Brainstorm Worksheets: These are special activities that will help you to implement the good ideas you've encountered in this book. You'll find them in Appendix B.

CRITICAL POINT #3:
YOUR ORGANIZATION NEEDS ROLE MODELS

After I finished writing *The Cult of Amazement*, I asked myself: What internal principles, beliefs, and best practices make a culture of Amazement possible? What are the standards that can ignite an Amazement Revolution within any size organization, whether it employs one person or thousands of people? Which companies are the very best role models for individuals and/or companies who want to make the transition to a cult of amazement? Drawing on decades of experience, I am offering this book as my answer to these questions.

I believe there are seven Amazement Strategies shared by the best service-focused organizations in the world. Much of this book is devoted to the true stories of these real-world role models, both people and enterprises who actually live by these Amazement Strategies and whose examples and best practices can help you transform your own workplace into that of a premier service organization.

The seven Amazement Strategies are:

1. **Provide membership.** We think of customers as members who deserve a superior level of service.
2. **Have Serious FUN.** We embrace *fulfillment, uniqueness,* and anticipation of what's *next* as internal operating principles.
3. **Cultivate partnership.** We deliver a level of service and create a confidence so compelling that customers might consider us a partner, not just a vendor or supplier.
4. **Hire right.** We hire the right people, and we look for the right personality for the job even before we look for technical skills.
5. **Create a memorable after-experience.** We deliver a powerful after-experience that reminds our customers how much they enjoy and appreciate doing business with us.
6. **Build community.** We create and support communities of loyal customers and employees, also known as evangelists.
7. **Walk the walk.** We operate under a clear, shared set of values that everyone throughout the entire organization understands and follows.

ABOUT THE ROLE MODELS

I selected fifty role models for this book. Many of these organizations will probably be familiar to you; some you won't recognize at all. I wanted a mix of role models, from small entrepreneurial businesses to large Fortune 500 companies, to show you that the Amazement Strategies can work for organizations of any size.

These role models have a lot to teach us about launching and sustaining a culture of amazement. With that said, I can only confirm that they are *currently* engaged in an Amazement Revolution. That doesn't mean they always were or will always be. As quickly as this book goes to print, one or more of these organizations might fall from grace. Furthermore, most of the role model companies don't practice all seven of the Amazement Strategies. That's good news for you because it proves that implementing just one or two of the strategies can put you on track, or keep you on track, to create an Amazement Revolution for your own customers and employees.

You may disagree with some of my role model choices. That's okay. (If you feel the urge to do so, please feel free to write me and tell me why you disagree.) Even though we may not see eye-to-eye about a company's role model credentials, I hope our differing views will not diminish the powerful lessons we can learn from these organizations.

To be included in this book as a role model, an organization had to:

1. **Demonstrate mastery** in at least one of the Amazement Strategies.
2. **Have a dedicated group of loyal customers or evangelists.** This is a real-world community from which the company draws praise and also ideas for improvement and innovation. You know your company is amazing when you've developed a community of evangelists!
3. **Show the ability to prosper, or at least rebound, during tough times in the larger economy.** Time after time, I have found that amazing companies use service, loyalty, and retention as critical marketplace weapons to survive and thrive during tough times.

Before we move on, I want to share a few important thoughts on the Amazement Revolution Takeaways (ARTs). First and foremost, I want to emphasize that what follows is not just a list of techniques. Here you will not only learn the important how-tos, but also some of the important whys behind a successful Amazement Revolution. Some of these ideas can be implemented immediately, and others will take a considerable amount of time to implement. Regardless of how long it takes to implement a given ART, you always want to look at what must happen to change the *culture* of the team or organization. I can teach someone the right strategy, but equally important cultural changes have to happen for someone on your team—or for your entire organization—to actually want to do the right thing by the customer.

I believe the best way to change the culture of an organization that's currently operating within the cult of uncertainty is to start treating employees the way you'd like customers to be treated—maybe even better. I call this the Employee Golden Rule, and it is at the heart of any successful Amazement Revolution. What happens inside the organization inevitably affects what happens to customers on the outside of the organization. Managers, that's the part of the Amazement Revolution that you must make a special effort to constantly pursue. It's all too easy, in the midst of our busy day, week, or quarter, to lose sight of the Employee Golden Rule!

Some managers who read customer service books like these are eager to the get tips they can share with the front-line team members that will help them improve interactions with customers, but they may be less interested in strategies to improve their own interactions with the team. The way managers communicate with their team members has far more impact on the level of service your organization delivers than any advice we pass along to them. As you make your way through this book, the seven strategies will not only help managers to improve your organization's relationships with customers, but they are also designed to help you support your employees, improve your relationships with *them*, and implement the Employee Golden Rule!

Managers must pay close attention to what is happening inside the organization, because the quality of their interactions with front-line people will determine the quality of the organization's interactions with customers.

The very first role model you will learn from—American Express—proves that any organization, including a global financial services giant, can make the Employee Golden Rule a driving operating principle of the enterprise. As you'll learn in the next chapter, constant improvements in the *internal* culture have made this company a global leader in the area of customer service.[3]

PART TWO

THE MASTER CLASS

CHAPTER THREE

THE MASTER CLASS: AMERICAN EXPRESS

In the chapters that follow, I spotlight each of the seven Amazement Strategies and offer operating examples and Amazement Revolution Takeaways (ARTs) from real-world organizations. To start, I want to give you a detailed "master class" in amazement by profiling, in depth, one world-class service organization that has led the way for the rest of us by implementing *all seven* of the Amazement Strategies throughout the enterprise and living them as operating principles on a daily basis. That organization is the diversified global financial services company American Express.

Amazement Revolutionary: American Express Company
Enterprise Focus: Financial services
Headquarters Location: New York, NY
Website: www.americanexpress.com
What You Need to Know: Founded in 1850, today American Express has over 58,000 employees. Famous for its credit card,

charge card, and traveler's cheque businesses, American Express cards deliver 24% of the total dollar volume of credit card transactions in the United States. *Business Week* ranks American Express as the twenty-second most valuable brand in the world; *Fortune* lists American Express as one of the top thirty most admired companies in the world; and as of this writing, J.D. Power and Associates has ranked the company as highest in customer satisfaction among credit card issuers for four consecutive years.

The selection of American Express as a primary role model is based on this organization's demonstrated record of service excellence (which has been verified by *Business Week*, J.D Power and Associates, and many other sources in recent years) and my own extensive research into the company's mission, culture, and operating principles. Once I had formalized the seven Amazement Strategies, my team and I did a great deal of research and undertook a series of detailed discussions with many key people within the company. After looking at hundreds of other businesses, our conclusion was that this organization is truly among the elite Amazement Revolutionaries. Very few established companies have completely internalized all seven of the basic Amazement Strategies we identified. American Express is definitely one of those companies!

What struck me was not merely the commitment of senior executives to raise American Express's game to a higher level, but the sheer speed with which a Fortune 500 company was able to mobilize and make the internal changes necessary to sustain and support an ongoing Amazement Revolution. As you will learn, the new internal initiatives that drove this revolution began only about five years ago.

Given the short timeline and high level of achievement, I believe American Express has successfully launched one of the most remarkable internal-service culture revolutions in the history of American business. As Jim Bush, the company's executive vice president of world service, is quick to point out, the changes that have played out in recent years are completely consistent with the company's 160-year legacy of service and innovation.[1]

As we spoke during our interview, I often got the feeling he and his team had been implementing precisely the same system I had been developing and refining over twenty-five years of work in the field of customer service! They had not been using my notes, of course, but rather implementing the same timeless strategies shared by all truly great service organizations. The core strategies go by many names. It's not what you call them that really matters, but whether you put them into practice.

Let's look at the seven Amazement Strategies now. You will notice that many of them, when followed to their logical conclusions, connect to and dovetail with other strategies on the list. Whatever names *you* give these ideas, you will find that they form an interlocking, self-sustaining set of core principles that are both easy to remember and easy to return to, day after day.

AMAZEMENT STRATEGY #1: PROVIDE MEMBERSHIP

Close-up on Membership

Shift your mindset to treat the people you serve more like *members* rather than *customers*. What would you do differently?

American Express doesn't have customers or users or clients. American Express has *members*. Every single holder of an American Express card is a "cardmember." Many of those members can quickly tell you, without even looking at the date on their card, exactly how long they've *been* a member. And the entire organization is oriented toward communicating with, engaging, and serving those members.

The specific concept of membership began in 1963, when American Express first began embossing those "member since" dates on their charge cards. The larger idea of defining a premium level of experience, one reserved exclusively for people who choose to work with American Express, really does have its roots in a premium-service ethic. "We're here to help," Bush told me. "That goes back to the start." That ethic has been part of the organization's legacy, and its chief competitive advantage, since the company's founding in 1850.

The American Express Company began life as an elite express shipping service. Back then, its role and mission was to "Forward Merchandise and Money, Collectibles with Goods, Notes, and Drafts, throughout the State of New-York, the Canadas, and all the Western States and Territories…Each Express in charge of a Special Messenger."[2] The service-driven company prospered—and innovated. In the 1880s it offered its mobile, worldly, generally upscale clients a revolutionary new solution to the frustrating personal challenge of not being able to make purchases easily while overseas: the traveler's cheque. The rest, as they say, is history.

In recent years, CEO Kenneth Chenault has reinvigorated the brand by inspiring a new generation of true believers to live up to American Express's lofty history—and its tradition of high service standards. Bush is one of those true believers. He proved that much during our conversation by returning over and over again to three critical themes that support the central service concept of membership as it is lived out every day at American Express.

Don't Think of Them as Customers—Think of Them as Members

"By putting that 'member since' date on our cards," Bush told me, "we create membership, and membership is something that our cardmembers treat as a badge of honor. It's not elitist. It's inclusive. It means they are appreciated, that they have the right, and expect, to be served in a premium fashion. As long as we *treat* them like members in high regard, we believe cardmembers will maintain their relationship with American Express. Our job is to continue to service the needs of all our customers who rely on us as a premium service experience organization.

"In fact," he continued, "we don't really think of ourselves as a credit card company at all. We actually view ourselves as a premium service company. We are really in the services business. We happen to facilitate payments. But it's the experience around those payments that makes what we do unique and special for our cardmembers."

What would happen if you stopped thinking of the people who do business with you as "customers" and started thinking of them—or even referring to them—as special individuals who occupied a special category? What would you do differently?

Offer Members Exclusive Amenities

A central part of the membership experience at American Express is being offered amenities that nonmembers don't have access to. "With the goal of membership in mind," Bush explained, "we offer the finest, most powerful rewards program in the world, with a host of rewards that emphasize the importance of membership."

Those rewards include access to fine dining through some of the company's premium card offerings, the ability to get tickets for exclusive theater engagements, and access to airport clubs for frequent travelers. Hundreds of other such amenities are tangible benefits of membership. And the sheer range of benefits American Express offers day after day, around the world has been impossible for other players in the credit card industry to duplicate. The right amenities can take the membership experience to another level, one that makes your enterprise unique.

What amenities could you offer people that are exclusive to working with you or would be difficult find to elsewhere?

Invest in the Membership Experience

Jim Bush repeatedly emphasized one point during our interview: American Express sees delivering premium service to its cardmembers not as an expense but as a critical strategic asset, one that pays back handsomely in both the immediate future and the long run. Accordingly, the company welcomes opportunities to invest in improvements in the quality of its membership experience.

"Service is the most powerful competitive advantage we have," Bush told me. "Service is not a cost, it is an investment. It's a growth engine for our company. Service is one of our most powerful channels of growth opportunity. Service is value creation. Service is using human interaction to enable mutual benefit, and not only are we willing to make that investment, we are really proud of our investments in service. In an age when service is perhaps at its lowest ebb, when there's basically a vacuum, regardless of where you go in the world, we're proud of the role we can play to fill that void. From our perspective, there's no time better than the present to capitalize on our greatest asset—by investing in the level of service that supports the experience we deliver."

No, this isn't just talk. When it comes to investing in the membership experience, Bush and his leadership team have been instrumental in making absolutely sure that American Express puts its money where its mouth is. As you will see when we examine the next Amazement Strategy, FUN, Bush and his team engineered a complete overhaul of the enterprise's training, recruitment, and customer service functions to lead an internal Amazement Revolution that has paid handsome dividends in the marketplace.

How can you invest in and improve your organization's membership experience?

! **ART #1:** Start thinking of your customers as members of a special group; consider a change in the labels you use to describe them, both internally and externally.

! **ART #2:** Brainstorm ways to deliver amenities that will take the customer experience to another level.

! **ART #3:** Invest in creating the membership experience.

AMAZEMENT STRATEGY #2: HAVE SERIOUS FUN

Close-up on FUN

Real FUN in the workplace is determined, not by how many belly laughs your enterprise generates, but by the level of *fulfillment* it generates in the workforce, the *uniqueness* it respects in each employee, and the sense of anticipation it creates for the *next* challenge on the horizon.

Leaders at many organizations—indeed, leaders at most organizations—pay lip service to the principle that customers "come first," are the "reason we're here," and so forth. Then those very same leaders continue an old habit: ignoring the real-world, day-in/day-out workplace experience of the employees who are supposed to deliver all that great service. It doesn't add up.

American Express's stated goal is to become the world's most respected service brand—and Bush and his management team knew that the company's legacy of service-driven innovation demanded a different approach. They knew that any successful revolution always begins from the inside.

Bush and his team launched that revolution using a strategic weapon I call Serious FUN. That's my terminology, not Bush's, but he and I are in complete agreement about the importance of the three elements I use to define workplace FUN: personal *fulfillment* in the job; a working environment that respects each employee's *uniqueness*; and a sense of escalating challenge that always leaves people looking forward to the *next* challenge, whether that means the next project, the next day at work, or the next rung on the career ladder.

By embracing all three of these values in its call center operations, American Express proves that a corporate giant really can create FUN in the workplace.

As Bush put it, "Sometimes people say, 'You've got to make people happy.' Well, we do want to stimulate people, but we want to give people the opportunity to be energized, to be engaged, in a way that will make happiness on their own terms possible. The goal is to not just make people happy as though they were simply being entertained.

"A lot of people are energized by a challenge," he went on, "which is great. But what we found was, for a while there, we were subsidizing poor performers, and that was as frustrating to the people on the team as anything else. By addressing all of that, we've created a highly engaged, very assertive workforce that's committed to both individual development and to achieving the collective objectives."

Faced with the task of reinvigorating its call center workforce, American Express used a novel tactic. It actually asked the people who worked in the call centers what was important to them.

"A few years ago," Bush explained, "we went out and we asked our front-line people questions. We asked: 'What is important to you to drive an experience that would get our customers to recommend American Express to a friend? What is required for you to be successful, for you to achieve your potential, for you to excel?' That survey mechanism went out to the front-line leadership, and to the people who were actually working on the front lines. The answers that came back covered five major themes. One answer was people wanted to be compensated fairly. Another was that they wanted to be recognized for the important role they play. A third response was that they wanted a career path and they wanted the opportunity to develop as professionals. Fourth, they wanted flexibility. They felt like they deserved not to be held to a rigid schedule, and they wanted flexible scheduling with their colleagues, so they could swap shifts to meet the ever-changing needs of their family life. And fifth, they wanted the tools necessary to be successful."

American Express senior management concluded those were all fair things to ask for. They have stayed focused on and continuously invested in those five aspirations, identifying and meeting the needs their front-line people identified.

"As part of the recognition of their concerns," Bush recalled, "we changed the job title. We said, 'Let's stop calling them reps. Let's stop calling them agents. Let's call them what they are.' And 'customer care professional' seemed to be more accurate as a title. We validated that through some focus groups with our front-line people. And that change in terminology has worked out very well."

Something else that worked out well involved a substantial financial investment: a complete overhaul of the call center priorities, from recruiting to training to compensation, in keeping with the request for better workplace tools and rewards. Bush made sure those changes happened.

To understand the Amazement Revolution that took place in his corner of American Express, you have to understand how impersonal and demotivating most call centers are for the people who work in them. Most call centers hire people with call center experience. These people are given metrics, and they are evaluated based on their ability to deliver those metrics. They're supposed to keep coming back to a certain script, or use the customer's name three times within the first sixty seconds, or keep the call under a certain amount of time, or talk to a certain number of people per hour.

Not surprisingly, when applied to a sea of potentially stressful calls with customers, standards like these burn out a lot of call center employees (and let's face it, a lot of customers, too). The turnover rate among employees at these call centers is quite high, often more than 100% annually.

American Express decided to take a different tack—by changing the hiring and recruiting philosophy (see Amazement Strategy #4: Hire Right, on page 35), by de-emphasizing the metrics, by training its people in generally unscripted "soft skills" such as listening and relationship building, and by investing in new technologies that enabled customer care professionals to make better customer-specific product and service recommendations during the calls. Instead of simply trying to shorten call times, the company made the strategic decision to use the calls to improve the quality of person-to-person connection with cardmembers. To do this, the company hired, trained, and motivated its customer care professionals to be better, more autonomous improvisers, a major change in workplace culture that gave front-line people much more control over the direction of the call.

"Three or four years ago, we spent 70% of our training on what screen to find and button to push," Bush said. "Now we spend 70% on how to service customers and how to work at a company with a service heritage like American Express. Anyone can learn the screens, but we're not in the screen business."

Since Bush and his team made these changes and others, American Express has seen a rise in cardmember awareness of its varied products and service offerings. That improvement has been accompanied by a strong upward trend in customers' overall satisfaction with the company. At the same time, the company's call center retention rates have improved. Turnover among these employees is now *below* the industry average!

Bush is certainly happy about these developments, but he doesn't seem greatly surprised by them. He appears to have virtually limitless faith in the transforming potential of an engaged workforce.

"By understanding that it's a people business first and foremost," he told me, "by investing in people, by creating performance management systems around those individuals that care for our customers, by defining what is right from a customer point of view and then rewarding the people who deliver on the outcome, we all learned that it's amazing what you can accomplish as an organization. As we started to develop a more autonomous and empowered environment, I think all of us felt a sense of release. We in management had not really created anything new, but we had *unleashed* the power of these incredible professionals. Now they're more than professionals, I think. They now pride themselves in being ambassadors of the American Express Company."

How could you make FUN a part of daily working
life at your organization?

! **ART #4**: Give your people a greater sense of personal fulfillment by giving them the training and the autonomy they need to solve problems and make good recommendations. Don't try to micromanage their every word and deed.

! **ART #5**: Respect and embrace the uniqueness of each of your employees.

! **ART #6**: Issue a professional challenge that inspires team players and makes them look forward to what's next.

! **ART #7**: Ask your team what should change.

! **ART #8**: Don't subsidize poor performance.

! **ART #9**: Throw away the script; give your people more autonomy to identify and solve problems.

! **ART #10**: Change internal job title terminology.

AMAZEMENT STRATEGY #3: CULTIVATE PARTNERSHIP

Close-up on Partnership

Deliver a premium level of service that incorporates active problem-solving and inspires customers to count on and return to your organization.

When American Express's customer care professionals not only take care of the initial reason for the call, but also empathetically ask about the cardmember's business, travel, or other issues, they are becoming *problem solvers.* True partnership often begins with this kind of proactive problem solving—which means not merely resolving the existing issue, but looking for other problems to solve in such a way that the customer begins to expect and rely on that level of care. This is partnership; this is where we want the relationship to go. And it begins with being empathetic, emphasizing shared values, and being fully accountable for the situation at hand.

"I think what we have been able to do successfully," Bush told me, "is use empathy to engage our employees in becoming part of the solution. That's the first step. They can actively listen, they can understand and empathize with the tone of the cardmember or the merchant or whoever we're talking with and attempting to serve; and through that assessment, they can determine then how the dialogue should go, listening for what's most important to the customer, and then engaging the customer through that. Even a simple apology early on can get us to a position where we can resolve the issue—and then we build from there. Once we've resolved the initial issue, then we start to look for opportunities to serve our customers beyond that interaction, opportunities that may help us to deepen the relationship.

"We are always building upon a solution—by reinforcing value opportunities and by creating incremental value. We try to do that with every interaction we have. And we have hundreds of millions of interactions every year."

In other words, once the customer care professional has worked with you to resolve your Moment of Misery, whatever it may be, he or she wants to use the positive emotional momentum of that experience to learn more about you—and find *more* problems to solve on your behalf. This high-level, aspirational partnership standard applies not only to American Express's relationships with its external customers but also to the company's relationships with internal customers (i.e., colleagues and coworkers) and, just as critically, with merchants (the vendor base). People within each of these groups have come to expect, not an absence of problems, but a higher level of problem solving from the American Express Company.

What if you viewed your customers' problems, crises, and Moments of Misery as opportunities to establish higher long-term customer expectations from your organization?

! ART #11: Empathetically solve existing problems. Then proactively look for unanticipated problems to solve.

! ART #12: Use crises and Moments of Misery as opportunities to build or expand the partnership.

! ART #13: Strive for partner relationships with customers, with your employees, and with your vendors.

! ART #14: Wherever possible, identify and emphasize core values you share with your partners.

AMAZEMENT STRATEGY #4: HIRE RIGHT

Close-up on Hire Right
Create and implement innovative hiring and retention processes that support your service mission.

American Express took a long, hard look at the way the enterprise was staffing its call centers and decided that the processes it currently had in place simply weren't keeping up with the competition. Contrary to what you might expect, though, its comparisons were not to the obvious competitors—Visa, MasterCard, or Discover Card.

The company chose to benchmark itself against organizations such as the Ritz-Carlton and the legendary Four Seasons hotels! So Bush and his team looked outside their own industry, to global leaders in the service field, for the hiring and retention processes they needed—and eventually they looked outside of their industry for the people they wanted to hire, as well.

As Bush put it: "We said, 'It's nice being the best in the credit card industry, but with all due respect, the credit card industry as a whole is not really viewed as being all that committed to service.' So we challenged ourselves: How do you look at other industries to learn from what they do, who they employ, and how they engage? And we made some changes."

Like other great service organizations I've worked with, American Express was willing to take a whole new approach to hiring and retention in order to deliver a better customer experience. Specifically, it was willing to recruit from an industry other than its own—the hospitality industry—and reassign or part ways with people who weren't predisposed to deliver the empathetic level of service that supported the company's mission.

"The fact that somebody has been in a call center," Bush said, "does not make that individual the perfect match for what we're trying to accomplish. Why? Because we're talking about human engagement, and that requires the ability to connect. And hospitality, when you think about engagement, that's exactly what those enterprises do."

That's how American Express began looking to a new profile for its customer-facing talent: direct customer-facing experience in service-driven hotels, restaurants, retail stores, and similar establishments. It began looking for an outgoing, empathetic, problem-solving attitude. Once it had identified the person who could support the organization's service-first culture, and who brought the right experience and the right outlook on customer care to the workplace day after day, the technical skills could be added to the mix.

There was also a comprehensive overview of the compensation structure, ensuring that one of its key drivers was customer feedback.

What would happen if you looked in places outside of your industry and identified a new career profile for your customer-facing service professionals?

! **ART #15**: Look outside your industry for good talent.

! **ART #16**: Don't be afraid to reassign (or part company with) people who don't belong in customer-facing positions.

! **ART #17**: Periodically reevaluate your compensation system. Consider making customer feedback one of the major drivers.

AMAZEMENT STRATEGY #5: CREATE A MEMORABLE AFTER-EXPERIENCE

Close-up on After-Experience

A positive initial customer experience is only the beginning! Make sure your organization gives people the flexibility to deliver a range of powerful, personalized *after-experiences*.

A while back, I called American Express and used their concierge service (a member amenity) to buy tickets for my mom to go to a Broadway show while she was on her vacation in New York City. I happened to mention to Tom, the customer care professional I was talking to, that the tickets were not for me. Tom immediately recommended that we set up the purchase so my mom could pick up the tickets at the ticket office in New York.

A few days later, I got a call back from the ticket merchant, updating me that Tom had alerted them to the fact that my mother would be stopping by the box office to pick up the tickets, and confirming for my convenience that this was the way I wanted the purchase set up!

Like a concierge at a great hotel, Tom had anticipated a potential problem and followed through. After he had hung up with me, Tom had foreseen that the box office might expect me to be present to pick up the tickets in person, which would have been a problem for my mother. (Typically, the member purchasing the tickets must pick them up and have the proper identification, which includes the same credit card used to charge the tickets and a driver's license or passport.) Tom had contacted the vendor and requested that the vendor circle back with me to confirm that the arrangement he and I had discussed was in place. Rather than hang up with me and move on to the next customer—make that *member*—Tom took an extra step. Tom was looking out for me!

Here's my question: What kind of working culture makes possible that kind of follow-through, that kind of positive after-experience?

The answer is, a working culture that doesn't focus narrowly on "transactions." Even after our call was completed, even after the "transaction" was over, I was still on Tom's radar. The "transaction" was only a small part of a more important relationship. And that is exactly how American Express wanted it.

This kind of person-to-person follow-through—which goes way beyond the now-familiar call from a credit card company to confirm that a big, unusual purchase is actually legitimate—is not simple altruism. It has a profound bottom-line justification, as Bush explains: "Follow-through is part of the larger strategy of relationship care. That's what really drives value for our organization, because it changes customer behavior in a number of positive ways: higher spending, faster payments from cardmembers, and an increasing number of merchants accepting the American Express card. All as a result of that person-to-person engagement with the customer care professional."

How can your organization use follow-through to create a memorable after-experience?

! **ART #18**: There is no such thing as a transaction. The word trans-action implies a clear starting point and an equally clear ending point. In the cult of amazement, however, any transaction is simply an interaction that leads to the next potential Moment of Magic.

! **ART #19**: Don't pressure employees to close customer interac-tions before they have a chance to build a relationship with the customer.

! **ART #20**: There are probably hundreds, if not thousands, of ways to effectively follow through. Empower people to find some of them. Recognize and consider rewarding them when they do.

AMAZEMENT STRATEGY #6: BUILD COMMUNITY

Close-up on Community
Support and inspire both the internal and the external community of evangelists.

American Express uses a powerful combination of incentives, emotional connection, and good listening to support two distinctive communities of American Express "evangelists": the internal community of American Express employees and the external community of cardmembers and merchants. Although these two communities are structurally very differ-ent, they are connected, and engaging on a person-to-person basis with members of each group is a central element of the company's mission. Each feels a sense of community and belonging, and a sense of identity, as a result of that engagement.

While we were discussing the loyalty and high retention rates of his community of customer care professionals, Bush shared with me his view that the larger mission of making American Express the world's most respected service brand has served as a powerful unifying force within the workplace. That mission, he said, had led to an important internal initiative: *to win customers' hearts and minds by delivering extraordinary care at the right margins.*

"These are more than just pithy words on a sheet of paper," Bush insisted. "This goal was internalized by tens of thousands of people who have passionately committed themselves to it. And the passion of our people is truly something remarkable. It's amazing what happens when you enable people to do what they're passionate about, how that translates into reality, both in terms of people's own ability to succeed as professionals and in terms of the experience they commit, as a community, to delivering to our customers."

In other words, the company's internal community of service employees is now mobilized and emotionally engaged around an inspiring service goal—a goal that they feel they own, one that gives them a sense of identity and belonging. Whenever that happens, in my experience, good things tend to follow in the external community of customers. And that is exactly the result that American Express achieved.

As far as that community of customers (make that *members*) is concerned, they too show a sense of belonging and identity, as evidenced by their active evangelism on behalf of the company. Consider the following post from an American Express member's personal blog, and notice how the first story involves a Moment of Misery that the company transformed into a Moment of Magic!

American Express is a great company. Not only have I been able to decorate my entire dining room using AMEX points, but I have had two recent experiences with AMEX that make me love them even more. A few weeks ago, (a family member's) car broke down at our house. I called the AMEX roadside assistance service, and they dispatched someone to come tow the car. I was still waiting after an hour and a half, so I called AMEX again to follow up. The woman I spoke with was so great—she said that it was unacceptable that I had waited over an hour for the tow truck and that she would send another tow truck to our house as well as follow up with the first guy. I truly felt like a valued customer and loved it!

If that weren't enough, I got a call on Friday from AMEX about a suspicious charge on my card. They had been monitoring my account and noticed that someone bought $488 worth of vitamins from an online vitamin distributor out of New Jersey. They had already suspended payment, and they closed my account in about 30 seconds over the phone. To top it off, I had a new card delivered to my door on Monday. Amazing! I know, I sound like a cheesy ad, but AMEX, you really are the best. I love you![3]

Here you see the member evangelizing about American Express—not only to immediate family and friends, but to a potentially global audience. All the advertising in the world could not be more powerful than that! Over the last few years, as I have noted, the company has been recognized for excellence in service by J.D. Power and Associates, *BusinessWeek*, and other institutions. It's worth noting that all of that recognition has been driven by the community of American Express members evangelizing on behalf of the company. The company did not apply for those awards! Central to all of that public recognition has been a service experience that inspires both loyalty and evangelism.

American Express creates and supports this community of evangelists via millions of interactions each year. Members' willingness to recommend American Express to family and friends appears to be driven by three powerful factors:

- A premier service experience
- The belief that American Express is willing and able to resolve problems when they arise

- The perception that the benefits offered by the company are superior to those offered by competitors

A 2010 J.D. Power survey of over 8,000 credit card users resulted in
five stars, the best possible rating, for American Express in each of those
three categories.[4]

"What more powerful marketing opportunity do you have," Bush
asked, "than when a customer refers you to a friend? That's the most powerful viral marketing there is."

***How can you deliver a service experience that creates a sense
of belonging and identity?***

! **ART #21**: Create goals that inspire and engage your internal evangelists (employees).

! **ART #22**: Develop value-added privileges, rewards, and amenities
to offer your customers as a way to build community.

AMAZEMENT REVOLUTION STRATEGY #7: WALK THE WALK

Close-up on Walk the Walk

Acknowledge, model, and reward adherence to customer-focused
values at all levels of the organization.

I like to describe the walk the walk strategy with the word *congruence*: the
customer-focused values you communicate to people should match up
with what you actually do. Other words that describe this state of being
are *authenticity* and *consistency*, but I prefer congruence because it does
a better job of conveying the crucial sense of values matching up, both
internally and externally. Congruence means you're doing something, not

because someone else told you to, but because doing it is what you genuinely believe to be right, and you are therefore willing to be accountable for your actions in all situations.

Congruence in an exchange with another person is an extremely powerful force that can turn around even the most challenging situation. The absence of congruence, on the other hand, signals inconsistency and opportunism and can do long-term damage to almost any relationship.

Congruence is what we all expect of, and sometimes actually get from, the people we rely on in life. Congruence is also a way of doing business. It's what truly great service organizations consistently deliver, whether or not there's a consumer problem to be resolved at any given moment. A lot of people mistakenly believe that the best service organizations have found some magic formula for *eliminating* problems altogether. That's nonsense. What these organizations have found, however, is the formula for *responding* to problems, whenever they arise, with full congruence.

And guess what? It works. The reason it works is that congruence, when combined with genuine empathy, is something consumers absolutely love to experience. They expect it from everyone, at every level of the organization, and when they get it, they look for reasons to stick around. When they don't, they look for reasons to leave. It's that simple.

Congruence is an institutional value first and foremost. Its presence or absence at all levels of the workplace—from the most senior employee to the newest hire—depends on the degree to which it has been modeled and supported by our leaders. The American Express world service leadership team's relentless emphasis on providing premium level service to all those who rely on the company wouldn't mean much if they didn't actually provide premium service to their own team, or if they didn't hold themselves accountable to the standard of actually winning the hearts and minds of cardmembers and merchants. They do.

If you want your employees to walk the walk, not just talk the talk, in their interactions with consumers, you must first walk the walk *in your own interactions with the team.*

I asked Bush how he measured individual and organizational progress toward the goal of "winning the hearts and minds" of consumers. The intensity and animation of his response instantly signaled to me that this was a topic near and dear to him. He offered me the powerful example of changes in the productivity metrics system at American Express, evidence of the service principle I call walk the walk.

"When you look at how we used to measure success historically," Bush recalled, "what you see is that we had a whole list of metrics that we used to track. We tracked how much time people spent on the phone, of course, but then we also had internal quality monitoring, which was much more subjective. We had checklists to evaluate whether the call was good or not, whether the engagement was good, and so on. The problem was, no two people would necessarily agree on what engagement was or what a good call was. Those metrics had nothing to do with customer feedback. So we said, let's eliminate that.

"We removed the subjectivity from our call evaluation system," Bush continued, "which meant we freed up the resources we'd been using to grade the calls. We then invested more heavily in our external surveys of customers, which we had been doing for a long time, but as a result of this decision to change the way we measured the success of a given call, we decided to generate the sample size necessary and the infrastructure necessary to extend the survey results all the way down to an individual customer care professional on the front line. That new measurement process asked one simple question: *Would you recommend American Express to a friend?*"

A side note: This now-famous survey query, which was developed by Fred Reichheld, is sometimes referred to as the Ultimate Question. Whatever you call it, though, the answers it generates tell you exactly how well the individual customer care professional is doing. By extension, that question also tells you exactly how well the *department as a whole* is doing. And that's not all: It also tells you exactly how well the *manager of the department* is doing! Once the manager publicly accepts accountability for the same standard he or she expects the team to meet, the whole dynamic of the workplace changes. People have something to model. What was once a *congruence vacuum* becomes a *congruence zone*!

"Now we are all, from me all the way across the world service organization, measured on the voice of the customer," Bush concluded. "We've made sure everyone's compensation, including mine, incorporates the driver of customer feedback. We apply the same principle up and down the line. That's a very important overriding objective in terms of driving outcomes."

Can you see where this is going?

The answer to the question "Would you recommend American Express to a friend?" ultimately tells you exactly how well *Jim Bush and the entire world-service management team* is doing! And don't think the people working on the front line don't notice the management team's willingness to embrace that standard. They do. They know the people they report to don't just talk the talk…they walk the walk.

How can you model congruence to the members of your team so they in turn can deliver congruence to your customers?

! **ART #23**: Model congruence with the right customer-focused values at all times.

! **ART #24**: Start a congruence movement within your organization. Everyone should walk the walk!

! **ART #25**: Identify customer feedback that's both objective and measurable that everyone in your organization, regardless of rank, can use as a benchmark.

! **ART #26**: Consider tying compensation to Fred Reichheld's Ultimate Question: "On a scale of one to ten, what is the likelihood that you would recommend us to a friend or associate?"

Now that you've seen one company that models all seven of the Amazement Strategies, both internally and externally, you're ready to look at some additional examples of organizations that have built one or more of these seven ideas into their mission. We'll take a look at them next, focusing on one Amazement Strategy at a time.

PART THREE
ROLE MODELS FOR AMAZEMENT

CHAPTER FOUR

STRATEGY #1:
PROVIDE MEMBERSHIP

Organizations that operate within the cult of amazement turn customers into evangelists by thinking of them as people with special status—as *members*.

Like many other world-class service organizations I've had the honor of working with, American Express launched its Amazement Revolution by thinking of customers in a whole new way. That was the essential first step. The result was a complete redefinition of the customer experience as a *membership* experience.

I'm not saying you have to use the word "member" or start a "membership program"—but I am asking you to start *thinking* of customers and other critical stakeholders as members, as people who have achieved special status by virtue of their decision to work with you. All of your customers are partners in your mission. The *concept* of membership, whether it is applied to a guest, a patient, or any other recipient of your service, must be central to your organization's customer service strategy, regardless of what you decide to call your customers.

The *membership experience* **has nothing to do with calling your customers "members." As long as you deliver your organization's unique membership experience, you can call you customers just about anything you want, assuming they like it!**

If you were to look at the people who buy from your enterprise, not as customers, but as members with elite status, how would you treat them differently? What would change in your organization's processes? In its communications, both internal and external? In its follow-through?

START WITH RECOGNITION, THEN ADD VALUE

Amazement Revolutionary: Four Seasons Hotels and Resorts
Enterprise Focus: Luxury hotel and resort chain.
Headquarters Location: Toronto, Ontario
Website: www.fourseasons.com
What You Need to Know: The first Four Seasons luxury hotel opened in London in 1970. Prior to that, the luxury theme had not been part of the Four Seasons brand, and the company was known primarily as a motel chain. In the years since that opening, however, the company has overseen more than eighty openings worldwide, and the properties it runs have been rated by sources such as Zagat and *Travel and Leisure* magazine as among the world's most elite upscale hotels, delivering a level of service that is unsurpassed. The chain has been named one of *Fortune* magazine's 100 Best Companies to Work For every year since 1998, when the list debuted.

I begin this section on membership with the remarkable example of the Four Seasons global family of luxury hotels. This premier service organization opens this part of the book for one simple reason: they create a *membership experience* within the first sixty seconds of a guest's check-in discussion more effectively than many of their competitors in the hospitality industry do over the course of a month-long stay. The Four Seasons staff gives their guests an instant feeling of inclusion, making them feel welcomed and special.

The membership experience is what happens when you consciously execute steps that consistently deliver to your customers a powerful, internalized sense of belonging, of having arrived at a "home away from home," of being in good hands. Identifying and delivering those steps is a fine art, and the processes that will deliver *your* enterprise's membership experience are likely to be quite different from those of any other enterprise. The steps you follow will, however, always deliver two deceptively simple-sounding principles: *recognition* and *unique value.* Those are the twin pillars of the membership experience.

Regardless of whether you call your customer a customer, client, guest, or use some other phrase, membership delivers recognition and a high level of value that is not easily available elsewhere.

An excellent example of a service experience that takes full advantage of both these pillars is the carefully designed guest-welcoming procedure used at the Four Seasons hotel chain. This process consistently creates a Moment of Magic within an engagement opportunity that some hotels (including some luxury hotels) manage to turn into a Moment of Misery: the first few moments of check-in. I travel a great deal, so I can tell you from personal experience that the check-in procedures business travelers endure can often send all the wrong messages: *I'm not here. I don't see you.*

Wait until I get off the phone. I'm too busy right now to look you in the eye. My time is valuable. Or even *I wish I were doing something else.*

The people who greet you when you check into a Four Seasons hotel never send you those kinds of messages, either verbally or nonverbally. Hiring the right people, however, is only half the reason the Four Seasons consistently gets check-in right. The other half of the equation is the *process* it trains its people to follow when engaging with a guest at the front desk. Let's take a look at that process now.

Here are the requirements an employee at the front desk of a Four Seasons hotel is trained to meet when checking in a guest:

- The receptionist will actively greet guests, smile, make eye contact, and speak clearly in a friendly manner.
- The receptionist will create a sense of recognition for each guest by using the guest's name in a natural manner and by offering a "welcome back" to return guests.
- The registration process will be completed within four minutes, including queuing time.[1]

Think of the last time you checked in to a hotel. Did the person who was serving you at the front desk meet these standards? Probably not. In fact, you may have felt just as anonymous *after* you had checked in as you did before!

The people at Four Seasons recognize that's what usually happens to us when we travel: we're treated anonymously. This "default setting" of feeling anonymous and unrecognized, which is the first and biggest obstacle to any membership experience, is exactly what the personalization of the Four Seasons check-in is designed to overcome. It starts with the receptionist's use of the person's name, authentically and sincerely, not robotically. In fact, Four Seasons uses a "three-R" mnemonic to help its team make the right kind of connections with guests, time after time: Recognition, Reassurance, and Respect.

Calling guests by their name in a friendly way ("Good morning, Ms.

Jones") is an integral component of the overall membership experience delivered *throughout* a guest's stay at a Four Seasons hotel. The check-in process establishes that high level of service for the guest, and it also establishes the happy expectation that it will be maintained. It *is* maintained, more often than not. That's amazement!

Look how carefully, and how wisely, the Four Seasons check-in process has crafted the *recognition* component of this critical greeting and welcoming process for the receptionist. A less experienced service company might have scripted out the number of times the guest's name was supposed to be repeated, and might also have scripted the words the receptionist was *always* supposed to say before and after the guest's name. Scripts, however, carry two big problems: they handcuff service people and leave them with no room to improvise, and they almost always sound insincere when delivered. The receptionist is given the *autonomy* to use his or own words to "actively greet" the guests and use the guest's name in a natural way.

I told you there are two pillars of the membership experience, recognition and value not easily attained elsewhere. Now that I've pointed it out, you can easily spot the recognition element. What about the high value? Is *that* actually being delivered during check-in?

It is. The people at Four Seasons have done decades of careful research on what people in their target market of wealthy business travelers value most highly. Can you guess what that commodity is? Here's a hint: It's not expensive wallpaper or fancy silver trays or pleasant background music or any other external aspect of the stay at the hotel.

It's *time*. These wealthy travelers consistently report to researchers that they are working harder and longer hours than ever before, that they experience serious stress in their lives because of the lack of available time to do everything they want to do, and that they flat-out resent being kept waiting. The Four Seasons does not keep them waiting, at check-in or anywhere else.

Look carefully at the requirements of the Four Seasons check-in experience, and you'll see that it is, above all, a message to guests that they have entered a special space where their time, whether it is to be used for work or leisure, is always regarded as a critical resource. The guest's time will *always* be respected. You don't have to waste time making an effort to catch the receptionist's eye; the receptionist actively greets you. That seemingly minor detail actually sends a whole series of very important unspoken signals: *I am here. I see you. You are the most important priority for me right now, and I am not putting any other task in front of the task of serving you.*

By sending these time-sensitive signals, and by completing the check-in process within that four-minute window, the receptionist is establishing a high level of service for the guest and setting the positive expectation that that standard will be maintained throughout the guest's stay.

Would it surprise you to learn that the Four Seasons always maintains a policy of 24/7 in-room dining? That its gift shops operate on special extended hours for the convenience of its guests? That it offers guests four-hour turnaround on dry cleaning? That these and similar amenities are all part of the hotel's long-term strategy for delivering value to its wealthy target market?

As Isadore Sharp, chairman and CEO of the chain, put it recently: "It became clear that the greatest luxury for our customer(s) was time, and service could help them make the most of that." That's a huge part of the value Four Seasons guests receive during every stay, and that stands out. These days, that level of respect for one's time is rare!

When you create processes that deliver personalized *recognition* to your customers, and you couple that with enhanced *value* that is difficult for your customers to obtain elsewhere, you create a special environment, a new world that your customers value, remember, identify with on a deep level, and want to return to. You create membership.

> ***How can you deliver a sense of recognition and value that sets you apart from your competition?***

! **ART #27**: Build processes that make your customers feel special by giving them recognition, reassurance, and respect.

! **ART #28**: Find out what your customers value most and find hard to get (such as time in the Four Seasons example). Build value-added "membership" offerings around that.

JOIN THE CLUB

Amazement Revolutionary: REI (Recreational Equipment Inc.)
Enterprise Focus: Outdoor gear and sporting goods retailer
Headquarters Location: Kent, WA
Website: www.rei.com
What You Need to Know: Founded in 1938, REI now has nearly 4 million members. The firm operates more than 100 retail outlets in twenty-seven states and opens four to six new stores each year. The firm employs over 9,000 people.

Hiking and sports apparel giant REI has over 10 million paid members—but it's happy to serve you even if you're not one of them. The privately held consumers' cooperative REI offers its own twist on the "membership has its privileges" concept by offering an accessible, consumer-friendly two-track service strategy. It sells outdoor recreation gear, sporting goods, and clothes to both members *and* nonmembers via catalogs, the Internet, and retail outlets.

Like American Express, REI prominently features "member since" dates on its personalized membership collateral. Unlike the American Express cardmember model, however, this company's model maintains two distinct customer bases: casual customers and paid members, who receive a host of benefits. The idea is, if you're not yet a member and you're part of the target audience of outdoor enthusiasts, you'll want to *become* a member before too long.

Lifetime membership, which costs just $20, entitles you to a special discount on all your purchases and a yearly dividend that can be taken either in cash or in the form of REI purchases. Other member benefits include major discounts on returned and lovingly used equipment (quite an advantage for serious outdoor experience aficionados), access to exclusive indoor climbing facilities, discounts on an extensive suite of in-person outdoor education programs, and a host of rental and service discounts. That's quite a payoff for a one-time fee of twenty bucks!

The two-track membership model has proved extremely successful. The firm's sales were recently in excess of $1.43 billion annually. REI's innovative business model is likely to be of interest to organizations that choose to emulate its two-track approach. This company, like American Express, has constantly excelled in implementing all seven of the Amazement Strategies and is a standout role model in at least two other areas: FUN (*Fortune* magazine includes the company in its Hall of Fame of great employers to work for) and community (because REI actively supports the environmentally driven values of its community of external evangelists).

The more you study this company, the more best practices you will gather.

Could your organization deliver membership benefits
so compelling that nonmembers want to upgrade
to experience those benefits?

!   ART #29: Consider a two-track service strategy that aims to turn casual customers into loyal members.

INDOCTRINATION

Amazement Revolutionary: Famous Dave's of America, Inc.
Enterprise Focus: Restaurant
Headquarters Location: Minnetonka, MN

Website: www.famousdaves.com

What You Need to Know: Famous Dave's is a restaurant chain specializing in barbecued ribs. It has 177 restaurants in 37 states. The chain has won over 200 awards for quality and service.

There really is a Dave, and he really is famous. The quirky restaurant chain that proudly sports the first name of Dave Anderson—an Ojibwe elder who once served as head of the federal government's Bureau of Indian Affairs—has earned a nationwide following of passionate barbecued ribs fans. (If you don't believe me, do an Internet search on the phrase "I love Famous Dave's.") Dave's many evangelists delight in singing the praises of the chain's succulent ribs and the unique, rustic atmosphere that turns every Famous Dave's location into a boisterous, family-friendly convention of rib and barbecue lovers.

Yet the ribs and the cool surroundings are only the most obvious half of this membership experience. The other half, the part you might not automatically associate with a rib joint, has to do with *indoctrination*. When you walk into a Famous Dave's, the service staff asks whether you've ever been to the restaurant before. If you haven't, they give you a mini tour of the place and show you how things work. That's a Moment of Magic in and of itself!

When you sit down, they put a marker on your table that indicates that you're a "first timer." You get a special, elevated level of service as an initiation message that shows you what's unique about the Famous Dave's experience. The quality of the food and the quality of the service continue to demonstrate *why* the diners who have been there before keep coming back.

If you're visiting for the first time, the people at Famous Dave's want to indoctrinate you. They want to bring you into their "inner circle," which is their overall dining experience.

***What would happen if you created an indoctrination experience
for your first-time customers?***

!   ART #30: Identify first-time customers and create a special welcoming or initiation ritual for them.

KEEP GOOD COMPANY

Amazement Revolutionary: The Better Business Bureau
Enterprise Focus: Consumer protection
Headquarters Location: Arlington, VA
Website: www.bbb.org
What You Need to Know: Founded in 1912, the Better Business Bureau operates 112 franchises in both the United States and Canada that coordinate their efforts through the umbrella organization known as the National Council of Better Business Bureaus. According to the organization's official Website, the Bureau's mission began in response to "medical quackery and the promotions of nostrums and worthless drugs."

One particularly successful variation on the membership experience leverages both the *recognition* pillar and the *benefit* pillar in a way that allows the customer to say, in essence, "Look at the kind of company I keep."

This *aspirational* membership experience, which may dovetail seamlessly with an existing membership-driven service process, is quite popular. It can be seen in many luxury brands (including the Four Seasons hotel family). Yet the common "snob appeal" description of these companies doesn't fully capture the essence of what is being delivered to their customers, which is much more profound: validation of their highest sense of self.

This kind of membership experience changes both the way we are perceived and the way we perceive ourselves. Consumers become *the kind of person* who uses an American Express card, *the kind of person* who stays at the Four Seasons, and so on. They prove to themselves *and others* that they belong in a group they are proud to be a part of. This is driven not so much by economic forces as by the desire to grow, improve, and excel, and it plays out on both the personal and the organizational level.

To illustrate the powerful appeal of this kind of membership experience, I want to showcase a company that delivers it, not to individual consumers, but to organizations: the Better Business Bureau. The Bureau is dedicated to a "Code of Business Practices" that "represents sound advertising, selling and customer service practices that enhance customer trust and confidence in business.[2] The code is built on the Bureau's Standards for Trust, eight principles that concisely describe important elements of creating and maintaining trust in business:

1. **Build trust**. Establish and maintain a positive track record in the marketplace.

2. **Advertise honestly**. Adhere to established standards of advertising and selling.

3. **Tell the truth**. Honestly represent products and services, including clear and adequate disclosures of all material terms.

4. **Be transparent**. Openly identify the nature, location, and ownership of the business, and clearly disclose all policies, guarantees, and procedures that bear on a customer's decision to buy.

5. **Honor promises**. Abide by all written agreements and verbal representations.

6. **Be responsive**. Address marketplace disputes quickly, professionally, and in good faith.

7. **Safeguard privacy**. Protect any data collected against mishandling and fraud, collect personal information only as needed, and respect the preferences of customers regarding the use of their information.

8. **Embody integrity**. Approach all business dealings, marketplace transactions and commitments with integrity. [3]

If you run a business, you certainly don't *have* to be a member of the Better Business Bureau to believe in these eight standards. You do have to be a member, however, if you hope to be *recognized by others* as having been certified by the Bureau for adhering to these guidelines.

Applying for Better Business Bureau accreditation means confirming, to your customers and the employees of your own organization, that you share in and are willing to be held accountable for these eight values; *winning* accreditation means you share the news with the outside world by means of the Bureau's famous torch logo. Notice that both internal and external factors combine to create this membership experience!

> *What would happen if you allowed your customers*
> *to leverage their "membership" experience to send*
> *a message to the rest of the world about their standards,*
> *values, and beliefs?*

! ART #31: Membership can allow your customers to send important messages about their values, traditions, and standards to the outside world. Build a "membership" experience that makes your customers want to say to themselves and others, "Look at the kind of company I keep."

PROVIDE A SENSE OF BELONGING

Amazement Revolutionary: Northern Lights Credit Union
Enterprise Focus: Financial services
Headquarters Location: Thunder Bay, Ontario
Website: www.nlcu.on.ca
What You Need to Know: Northern Lights Credit Union is a full-service financial institution operating eight offices in Northern Ontario; its stated core values are "innovation, fiscal responsibility and member-driven quality service."[4]

If you ever find yourself talking to someone who works at a credit union, don't make the mistake of calling the people who use the credit union's services "customers." You'll be quickly and enthusiastically corrected. Those people are not customers; they're members!

Membership is the driving concept behind every credit union. Account holders are technically shareholders in the enterprise, and they have both a stake in the institution's success and a say in its operation. To become a member, you generally need some kind of local affiliation, such as being employed by a company that's a member or living in a certain geographic area. Some credit unions leverage this strong local orientation into a powerful competitive advantage by making membership in the community more or less synonymous with membership in the credit union. In essence, they employ a grassroots marketing strategy that appeals to you to join the credit union and enjoy its benefits because you are already practically a member of the family.

Northern Lights Credit Union, which operates eight branches in Northern Ontario, offers Pay-for-A's, one of my favorite campaigns operating on a grassroots principle. Local high school seniors who are members in the credit union can bring can bring their report cards and photo ID into any Northern Lights Credit Union branch to receive $10 for every A on their most recent report card! As if that weren't enough, every A also entitles students to a ticket in the annual Pay-for-A's raffle to win the grand prize of a new laptop computer.

This program delivers the fundamental member benefit of *recognition*. Local students are rewarded for scholastic excellence, which makes excellent dinner table conversation focused on the student—and great word-of-mouth advertising for the credit union. Every student who participates gets not only personalized service (a benefit), not only cash (another benefit), but also sustained recognition from family and friends on a personal level. One A student every year gets even more recognition, in the form of local news coverage, additional attention from friends and loved ones, and a brand new laptop to take to college. Through it all, the credit union makes even deeper inroads into the community it serves, and it establishes major competitive barriers to other organizations (banks, for instance) that provide essentially the same services.

Could your organization share good news about your customers with other customers, with the people in your community, or even with the rest of the world?

! **ART #32**: Introduce customers to your organization by appealing to a powerful sense of belonging. This is not just good customer service, it's also good marketing!

GRANT ACCESS

Amazement Revolutionary: Entrepreneurs' Organization (EO)
Enterprise Focus: Membership organization supporting entrepreneurs
Headquarters Location: Montgomery, VA
Website: www.eonetwork.org
What You Need to Know: The Entrepreneurs' Organization was founded by a band of young entrepreneurs in 1987. The group describes itself as a "dynamic, global network of more than 7,500 business owners in 38 countries."[5] Members must have annual revenues of at least $1 million and have ownership or controlling interest in their company.

The Entrepreneurs' Organization's tagline—"for entrepreneurs only"—perfectly captures both the organization's mission and its formula for amazement. EO's organizational goal is to serve as "the catalyst that enables entrepreneurs to learn and grow from each other, leading to greater business success and an enriched personal life."[6] When you become a member of this "club," you get something nonmembers don't have: *access.*

Specifically, you get access to others in the network, in the form of your own personal board of advisors. You get access to information and resources unavailable anywhere else, including an experience-rich peer group database that leverages the insights of over 25,000 experts. You also get access to an impressive roster of global thought leaders who make personal appearances at EO chapters around the world. In the past, these thought leaders have included Richard Branson, George Bush, Colin Powell, and many other high-profile world and business leaders.

EO is a true membership organization. You pay to belong. You have to qualify to belong. Still, EO considers their members to be their customers, just like any other business. They have a value proposition for which their members are willing to pay. A big part of that value is the access to people and information that most of the general public will never have access to. That's what makes being an EO member special.

*What special access can you grant your customers just
for doing business with you?*

! **ART #33**: Make access to hard-to-get resources, people, experience, ideas, and tools a benefit of doing business with you.

WELCOME THEM TO THE CLUB

Amazement Revolutionary: Sports Clubs Network (Sports Clubs)
Enterprise Focus: Health clubs
Headquarters Location: New York City, NY
Website: www.mysportsclubs.com
What You Need to Know: Sports Clubs operates over 155 fitness centers in New York, Boston, Philadelphia, and Washington DC, as well as facilities in Switzerland. Total membership is over 483,000. The parent company is TSI Holdings.

One of the main points I've tried to convey in this section of the book is that *thinking differently* about your customers is the first and most important step when it comes to implementing the membership concept. If you start *thinking* of the people who buy from you as members, and then *treating* them as members, you'll be on the right track. You don't necessarily have to call your customers "members," and you don't have to call the place where you sell them whatever it is that you sell them a "club." But you should know that if you do, you'll be in awfully good company!

Sports Clubs operates the largest private network of athletic clubs in the northeastern United States. If you live in New York, Boston, Philadelphia, or Washington DC, you've seen their trendy workout facilities, which are branded as (you guessed it) New York Sports Club, Boston Sports Club, Philadelphia Sports Club, and Washington Sports Club. The simple fact that they've branded the chain as *clubs* and actively refer to their customers as *members* helps to send the right internal and external messages—and create the membership experience.

All that's really happening at these facilities is that customers are working out. They could do that at any number of places. But they choose to do it at one of the Sports Clubs *because of the expectations that the "membership" standard has created* and because of the way those expectations, over time, have been fulfilled.

You'll notice that each of the companies in this section has put its own twist on their organization's unique membership experience; Sports Clubs is no exception. It provides access to their clubs and programs, such as specialized classes, personal training programs, a series of escalating rewards for the most devoted customers (including a suite of premiere training facilities set aside for high-level "members"), and yes, a certain status appeal in the form of licensed apparel that instantly sets one apart from less-committed workout aficionados. But what drives all of these elements of the Sports Clubs' experience? The words *member* and *club*. These carefully chosen words keep both staff and customers on target, and they are hardwired into the organization's culture.

Disney calls its park visitors "guests" and uses that word as a constant reminder that the organization is committed to deliver a specific level of service. Sports Clubs calls its customers "members" for much the same reason—and gets comparable results.

What could you call your customers—besides "customers"— to create a strong positive expectation from the membership experience? How would your organization fulfill that expectation?

! **ART #34**: Make changes in your organizational terminology with words like "member" and "club" that will help keep both staff and customers focused on expectations of a high level of service.

RECAP: AMAZEMENT STRATEGY #1—PROVIDE MEMBERSHP

To implement this Amazement Strategy, try these ideas:

- Launch your very first interaction with the customer with personal recognition and then add value, as the Four Seasons chain of hotels does.
- Give customers a special "membership track" to join so they can get even more value from the organization, as REI does.
- Indoctrinate first-time customers with a great first-time experience, as Famous Dave's does.
- Help your customers send a message to the rest of the world about their values, standards, experience, status, or ethics, as the Better Business Bureau does.
- Give customers a sense of belonging, as Northern Lights Credit Union does.
- Make access to resources, people, experience, ideas, and tools a benefit of doing business with you, as the Entrepreneur's Organization does.

- Call your customers something besides "customers," as Sports Clubs does.
- Key point: Treating your customers like members doesn't mean you have to *call* them members. It's about creating value, similar to what some might call a "member benefit." Creating that sense of membership is a powerful strategy to deliver amazing service and establish customer loyalty.

CHAPTER FIVE

STRATEGY #2:
HAVE SERIOUS FUN

Organizations that operate within the cult of amazement have employees who look forward to coming to work every day. Why? Because their personal sense of *fulfillment*, of being appreciated for their *unique* needs and skills, and their anticipation of the *next* challenge supports and motivates all their interactions with customers. This FUN is essential, because what is happening on the inside of the organization is always going to be felt by the customers.

Is your company FUN to work for?

I'm not talking about how often you go to a company picnic, or take a trip to a barbecue joint with the sales team, or spend time at an arcade where everybody on staff gets to play video games. I'm talking about FUN, which is all about engaging the workforce by supporting *fulfillment*, *uniqueness*, and the *next* professional challenge on the horizon.

Ideally, every employee in the enterprise should be able to have this kind of FUN. If someone's not engaged enough to have FUN, that means the company is not yet operating completely within the cult of amazement—and that means relationships with customers will suffer.

When you first saw American Express's name linked up with the idea of FUN in an earlier chapter, were you a little skeptical or at least a little curious? American Express incorporates the FUN principle by listening to employees, using their input in constructive ways, and giving them the flexibility and the autonomy they need to do their jobs well. That's a different kind of FUN.

There are plenty of ways to have FUN that don't have anything at all to do with parties and laughing and cracking jokes.

Years ago, at one of my speaking engagements, I met a gentleman who worked in the medical equipment field. Enthusiastically, he told me what he did for a living (he was in sales). Then he said, "If you don't work for a hospital, then you've never heard of my company, or at least I hope you've never heard of us. The only way you would be familiar with our equipment is if you were dying!" As serious as the equipment he was selling was, it was obvious to me that he loved selling his product and enjoyed working for his company. I believe that his love of his work eventually reached all of his prospects and customers.

There's a saying that if you do what you love, you'll never work a day in your life. If you want the members of your team to do what they love and to share that sense of engagement with your customers, then you must be ready to focus on three elements of true workplace FUN. These are the same three elements that American Express has made an operational priority: the level of *fulfillment* the workplace generates, the *uniqueness* it

respects in each employee, and the sense of anticipation for the *next* challenge on the horizon that it creates.

Serious FUN is not an afterthought, not a one-time party theme, not an excuse for an off-site gathering once a year. It's part of the long-term strategic plan at every truly customer-focused organization. That's because building a customer-focused operation is simply impossible if you don't first focus on the team! FUN is not always expressed in laughter, although it certainly *can* be expressed that way. The real question is, will your customers sense the FUN that's built into your company's DNA?

SERIOUS FUN: ENGAGE YOUR EMPLOYEES, AND THEY WILL ENGAGE WITH YOUR CUSTOMERS

Amazement Revolutionary: Baptist Health South Florida
Enterprise Focus: Health care
Headquarters Location: Coral Gables, FL
Website: www.baptisthealth.net
What You Need to Know: The Baptist Health South Florida hospital system is an award-winning health care provider with a nationally recognized tradition of delivering great service to its patients. Its Miami facility was given a Consumer's Choice award fourteen years in a row! The network employs approximately 13,000 people.

Brian E. Keeley, president and CEO of the award-winning Baptist Health South Florida hospital network, has launched nothing less than an Amazement Revolution in the health care sector. Keeley says, "We strongly believe that the health and well-being of our employees is critical to our ability to care for our patients."[1] Starting with that refreshing foundation principle, Keeley's stated aim is for his organization to be a "destination employer"—the kind of company employees seek out and go out of their way to remain with. "As a destination employer," he says, "when I talk to people during orientations, I tell them I want them to spend the rest of their career here."[2] Why? So *patients* will receive a better experience!

Keeley himself has logged thirty-five years with the hospital network and its legacy institutions, but the scale and focus of his work makes it clear that it's not seniority for seniority's sake that he's after. He is focused not just on employee retention, but on employee engagement—on what I call FUN—because doing so is a critical part of the long-term Baptist Health strategic plan.

That core idea might at first glance seem like simple common sense for anyone working in the field. Of course health care providers should recruit, inspire, and retain the best talent for as long as possible. That way, few patients will encounter caregivers who are on the wrong side of a learning curve, and more patients will be able to build long-term relationships with the people who take care of them. That's what happens at Baptist Health South Florida. As Keeley puts it, "As a result of seeing the same faces every time they come in, our patients are greatly pleased to have such an intimate service delivered to them by people they know."[3]

Yet, common sense or not, this is a service model that most other health care organizations (indeed, most organizations in all industries) have failed to implement. Why? One big reason is that hospitals have yielded to the temptation to lay off staff during periods of economic challenge—and have alienated the remaining employee base. So far, during Keeley's tenure, Baptist Health South Florida has found the discipline (and the conservative fiscal management) to say no to layoffs and to put employees first. In fact, since its founding in 1990, the health network has *not once* implemented a layoff; to the contrary, it recently launched an initiative called the Baptist Health Way, which amounted to a corporate commitment to give employees competitive compensation, long-term job security, and a positive atmosphere in the workplace. Keeley oversaw this initiative in the midst of a major global economic slowdown!

The Baptist Health Way initiative is part of the organization's remarkably up-front commitment to avoid traumas like layoffs, rumors of layoffs, and salary cutbacks. "People never forget," Keeley observes. "Treat your employees badly and they don't forget it after the first six months or year. They remember it forever."[4]

Judging by the company's retention rates and the positive reviews it receives at anonymous evaluation Websites like glassdoor.com, the strategy is working, and the sense of commitment is mutual. Members of Baptist Health's senior management, according to Keeley, stay on for an average of ten to fifteen years, an astonishing figure in this volatile employment sector. The loyalty is not limited to senior executives. Baptist Health has been listed as one of the highest-ranking employers in America in terms of overall workplace satisfaction;[5] its nursing turnover came in at 10%[6], lower than the national average.[7] On a similar note, a major national survey of physicians identified South Miami Hospital—one of Baptist Health's flagship facilities—as one of the top three hospitals in the entire country in the area of physician satisfaction.[8]

Even so, the word "satisfaction" is misleading; satisfaction is not what Keeley talks about, and it's not really what he is after. His vision is one of selecting, recruiting, and *engaging* (not merely satisfying) a base of great employees. That people-first vision is central to everything that happens at Baptist Health South Florida. According to Keeley, "It starts with people. And it ends with people....It starts with attracting world-class physicians, getting the nurses, the skilled technicians, and everybody that works around the patients. From the highest-skilled neurosurgeons to the lowest-skilled food service people, it all starts with the people."

"It starts with people." Brian Keeley's driving operational philosophy —find the best people and keep them engaged enough to stay—is the foundation upon which Baptist Health South Florida's stellar reputation for patient amazement has been built.

In Keeley's world, as in everyone else's, high turnover is one of the mortal enemies of amazement, both internal and external. And engagement is

Keeley's weapon of choice when it comes to combating that turnover. The question is, how does he make it happen? The answer: FUN.

Baptist Health South Florida offers its employees *fulfillment.* This employer is a relentless supporter of growth for its employees, both personal and professional. This support takes the form of some eye-popping education benefits that a lot of companies would dismiss as too expensive: ongoing in-house and out-of-house educational programs, for instance, and even some generous scholarships for employee children. Yet low-cost, high-creativity programs seem to be just as important elements of the fulfillment mix. The Baptist Health South Florida workplace is one of escalating personal and professional challenge; that means self-selection of work assignments and environments for many employees. High tech or high touch? Caregivers often get to choose. In return for a greater say in what their working environment looks and feels like compared to what they would get at a competing hospital, employees accept workloads that are above the industry average.

Baptist Health South Florida respects each employee's *unique needs and expectations.* Again, this commitment takes the form of investments both financial and creative. There's an organizational commitment to flexible, easily accessible childcare. It's available in the workplace, as an off-site option, or even in one's home. The offerings here are either free to employees or incredibly cheap, and they are so robust and so easy to tailor to individual employees' lifestyle demands that the organization has won numerous awards for its childcare programs alone. *Working Mother* magazine regularly names Baptist Health South Florida as one of the most mom-friendly workplaces in the country. Given that 75% of the network's roughly 13,000 employees are female, that's a nice accolade to have! Before anyone in your organization dismisses such an employee-specific support program as unaffordable, raise this question: Can a major hospital network—or any other organization, for that matter—"afford" to have three-quarters of its workforce distracted by uncertainties about their personal childcare commitments during the course of the average work day?

What about low- or no-dollar investments in the unique needs and expectations of employees? Baptist Health South Florida offers plenty of those, as well. Support of flex time is a major management priority within the organization; employees can create work schedules that meet their own needs, and shift-swapping is an established practice among doctors and nurses.

Giving employees a sense of personal control over their own working day actually "costs" senior management little or nothing.

Baptist Health South Florida motivates its employees to look forward positively to what's *next* at work. Alienation and disaffection from the company mission are rare among employees here. A big reason for this is Keeley's realization that people only look forward to their work when they are challenged by it.

Accordingly, he measures (and manages using) the metric of employee engagement. As he points out, "Engagement is a term that implies not only [that] people like their work, but [that] they're challenged at work. They're psychologically, mentally, and physically challenged."[9] When an employee isn't challenged, it's time to look at new options!

Serious FUN requires meaningful communication between management and all employees, and particularly front-line employees who have the responsibility to interact with customers. Not surprisingly, Baptist Health South Florida is a national role model in this regard, as well. A special employee council has regular contact with senior management, including the CEO. And Keeley himself has regular face-to-face "town meetings" with employees in all the network's major facilities.

Ultimately, FUN—fulfillment, unique needs and expectations, and positive anticipation of what's next—must deliver a positive customer experience. Baptist Health South Florida's record of achievement proves that is possible on a large scale! As usual, Brian Keeley has the best explanation for why that is: "If we have happy, productive, committed, passionate employees, we know we're going to do a great job providing absolutely superb clinical care with a very high service component."

Are people at your organization having so much FUN that they consistently want to deliver a great service experience?

! **ART #35**: Once you engage your team with FUN by giving them work that is fulfilling, that utilizes their unique talents, and that is challenging, they will engage with your customer service mission.

! **ART #36**: Engage your employees the way you want them to engage your customers, and you will start to create employee loyalty.

GET TOGETHER

Amazement Revolutionary: Alston & Bird LLP
Enterprise Focus: Law
Headquarters Location: Atlanta, GA
Website: www.alston.com
What You Need to Know: Founded in 1893, Alston & Bird employs about 900 attorneys in nine cities throughout the United States. The firm has been named to *Fortune* magazine's list of 100 Best Companies to Work For multiple times.

FUN means making absolutely sure the workplace community gets engaged and stays engaged. One of the outstanding role models for this kind of group engagement is Alston & Bird, an Atlanta-based national law firm. Named one of the best places to work in America by *Fortune* magazine for nine consecutive years, Alston & Bird has raised internal communication to an art form.

Monthly all-team meetings update, motivate, and inspire each and every one of the firm's employees, no matter where they work or what they do. Each month, Alston & Bird's nine far-flung offices come together virtually, by means of videoconferencing, for a real-time full company gathering. These meetings are used to bring everyone up to speed on the latest news, to introduce new members of the team, and to instill and support a sense of community among contributors at all levels.

In addition to the monthly gatherings, employees stay connected by means of briefings from senior partners, "town hall" meetings, a daily online newsletter, and even special events designed to introduce recent hires to their new colleagues. It's all part of supporting social interaction in the workplace, which is a big component of *fulfillment* and a critical element of the FUN equation.

Alston & Bird uses deeply embedded traditions of open discussion and interaction to create a sense of belonging at all levels. "Everyone here—from those in the mailroom to the senior partners—feels valued. That's very important to our culture,"[10] says Michael Nutter, a manager at the Atlanta office.

Richard Hays, Alston & Bird's managing partner, sees the monthly meetings as important tools for enhancing and improving internal con- nections within the firm—connections that improve client service levels. "So much of what we do is relationship driven," Hays observes. "So the stronger those relationships are, the stronger we are as a partnership." [11]

What are you doing to stay connected to all of your employees?

! **ART #37**: Use regularly scheduled all-team meetings to energize and connect with everyone.

GIVE PEOPLE ROOM

Amazement Revolutionary: Google

Enterprise Focus: Internet search engine services, advertising, computer software

Headquarters Location: Menlo Park, CA

Website: www.google.com

What You Need to Know: The world's premiere search engine, Google provides its users with a wealth of supporting tools, including Gmail and Google Docs. The company, which employs over 23,000 people, was founded in 1998 and generates over $23 billion in annual revenue.

Did you know that search engine giant Google wants its engineers to take 20% of their work time—one day a week—to focus on company-related projects of their own design? The idea is that people will be more productive when they're working on something they are personally devoted to. Guess what? They are!

Many managers would feel a little uneasy yielding one-fifth of a critical employee group's available time to unscheduled, unstructured time. By freeing up this time, however, Google has been able to develop some of its most popular and strategically important applications. These include Gmail, the free, flexible, easy-to-use e-mail application that serves millions of people; Google News, the search-driven news engine; and parts of Google Reader, the popular aggregator of news feeds and blogs.

The driving idea behind the policy now known as "20% time" is that people who come up with great ideas are given the opportunity to explore them. The projects they take on may involve a single new product, or they may involve large-scale internal changes that affect the way whole chunks of Google operate. In some cases engineers work on their own during their 20% time; in others, they combine their 20% time with others, pooling their ideas, their enthusiasm, and their support for a new way of doing things.

As Google engineer Bharar Mediratta put it, "Google works from the bottom up. If you have a great technical idea, you don't have your VP send out a memo telling everybody to use it. Instead, you take it to your fellow engineers and convince them that it's good. Good ideas spread fast, and this approach keeps us from making technical mistakes. But it also means that the burden falls upon you to spread your idea."[12]

The 20% time policy gets people invested in good ideas—and it also gives them a powerful sense of *fulfillment* deriving from their lead role in the new concepts being developed. The policy supports needs, aspirations, and expectations that are *unique* to the individual. And it certainly gets people looking forward, in a positive way, to their *next* opportunity to work on their idea of choice.

Should every organization implement this concept with every employee? Probably not. Could *someone* in your enterprise create the next breakthrough product or service as a result of being allowed to work a certain amount of time each week on self-chosen projects? Absolutely!

Are you willing to let your employees do what they want to do and what they're great at, at least part of the time?

! **ART #38**: Give your most creative people the opportunity to spend at least part of their time on projects they choose that will also create value for the customer. This approach focuses on the employee's uniqueness. As a result, you will have more engaged and fulfilled employees—and that's good for business!

BE FLEXIBLE

Amazement Revolutionary: Slalom Consulting
Enterprise Focus: Consulting
Headquarters Location: Seattle, WA

Website: www.slalom.com

What You Need to Know: Ranked by *Consulting* magazine as one of the best consulting firms to work for in the United States, Slalom Consulting has also been recognized by the National Association for Business Resources (NABR) as a company with "exceptional commitment to innvative human resource initiatives that positively benefit employees."[13] Founded in 2001, it now employs over 800 people.

What would happen if your most creative employees set their own hours and dictated their own "face time" requirements for how much time they need to spend in the workplace? The record of Seattle-based Slalom Consulting suggests that the answer to that question is a record of strong growth in a highly competitive marketplace; a sustainable tradition of productivity, creativity, and innovation; and the ability to secure and hold on to the very best people.

According to the business and technology consulting firm, which has satellite offices around the country, what sets Slalom apart is its "consultant-built and consultant-led culture," a culture consciously designed to ensure "work and life equilibrium for all of [Slalom's] employees." The organization's progressive employment practices include the ability to work from home, coworker sabbaticals, and (most alluring for potential new hires) the total absence of unwanted travel demands.

That last item is rare indeed in the consulting arena. In fact, most top-tier consultants at Slalom's competitors come to view their perpetual "road warrior" lifestyle as a major obstacle to a harmonious family life and a reason to leave their lucrative, but stressful, positions. Slalom's innovative, self-designed workplace model is thus not only a perk for its current employees but also a major strategic advantage when it comes to attracting and retaining top-notch talent.

As general manager for Slalom's Chicago branch Tom Snapp put it, "Our consultants and leadership are one and the same—professionals empowered to realize their potential whether they are working with clients or enjoying life outside of the office."[14] Slalom's emphasis on autonomy and a self-directed workflow "eliminates cross-country travel and, for the first time, makes it possible for consultants to sleep in their own beds as opposed to living out of suitcases and hotels—as is common for employees of more traditional consulting firms."

Slalom offers the "best and the brightest" something that most consulting operations *don't* offer: FUN. That means giving employees *fulfillment* on their own terms; respecting their *unique* needs and expectations; and supporting the kind of engagement that gives them a reason to look forward to—instead of dread—the *next* assignment. That creates a better relationship with the company—and with the customer!

Are you listening to what your employees are saying about work/life balance?

! ART #39: Build and support a culture that supports flexibility in the workplace. This flexibility could express itself in terms of scheduling, working from home, or even the décor in an employee's workspace. Leverage this culture to attract and retain the best talent.

CREATE A PEER RECOGNITON PROGRAM

Amazement Revolutionary: Thomas Interior Systems, Inc.
Enterprise Focus: Office furniture
Headquarters Location: Bloomingdale, IL
Website: www.thomasinterior.com
What You Need to Know: Founded in 1977, Thomas Interior Systems offers 300 lines of office furniture products and a full range of services including space planning, installation, and ergonomic assessments. The company was named one of the "Best Places to Work in Illinois" by Best Companies Group.

In a recent interview, Thomas Interior CEO Tom Klobucher described the company's mission this way: "We don't sell furniture. We sell great places to work."[15] That comment alone suggests how important employee fulfillment is in Klobucher's business model. The use of the physical workplace to deliver fulfillment extends not just to Klobucher's external customers, however, but also to his internal customers, the employees.

When an employee at Thomas Interior Systems does a great job, everyone in the office knows about it. That's because Thomas has created special thank-you cards to acknowledge and celebrate above-average employee accomplishments. Anyone in the organization can fill out and send one of these cards to anyone else; the only criterion is the person on the receiving end has to have done something truly special to make an internal or external customer happy.

When employees receive one of these cards, they post it prominently in their cubicle for all the world to see. There's a lively ongoing competition to see who can accumulate and display the most thank-you cards.

How can you showcase, celebrate, and reinforce examples of great customer service?

! **ART #40**: Create a program for employees to recognize, acknowledge, and reward their peers for superior service. Encourage employees to display the cards they receive in their work area. This kind of public praise creates a sense of fulfillment!

TRUST IS NONNEGOTIABLE

Amazement Revolutionary: SAS Institute, Inc.
Enterprise Focus: Computer software
Headquarters Location: Cary, NC
Website: www.sas.com

What You Need to Know: The acknowledged leader in business analytics tools, SAS's most prestigious accolade, among many others, may be being named in 2010 as the number one entry in *Fortune* magazine's list of 100 Best Companies to Work For. The firm was founded in 1976 and today employs over 11,000 people.

The privately held software firm SAS, which makes sophisticated analytics tools used by organizations ranging from Victoria's Secret to the US military, has the reputation of being one of the best places on Earth to work.

SAS's richly deserved great reputation for employee relations is usually attributed to the most obvious *tangible* evidence of the company's commitment to its employees. That would be those jaw-dropping perks you may have read about: the country club; the vast gym, complete with masseur; the day care; the on-site health care; the free M&Ms every Wednesday; and on and on. The firm's broad menu of employee benefits is impossible to ignore, and that is both a blessing and a curse to those interested in learning what works and why at SAS. It's a blessing because it shows how well a world-class employer treats its people; it's a curse because it seems to suggest that the key to success lies in bribing employees to stay.

In reality, bribery is *not* the edge this innovative employer brings to the marketplace. The real competitive advantage SAS has harnessed lies in something intangible: the internal culture of trust. That culture of trust is what keeps SAS people *fulfilled*, what keeps them satisfied in their own *unique* needs and expectations, and what keeps them committed to addressing the *next* personal and organizational challenge they face in the workplace.

Jim Davis, SAS's senior vice president and chief marketing officer, puts the matter eloquently: "Our culture is a result of a deliberate, dynamic strategy that is founded on three fronts: trust, flexibility, and very strong core values." One powerful example of the trust SAS has in

its employees is its ongoing commitment not to lay them off—a promise the company has so far been able to keep, even in tough economic
times. Another indicator of the high level of two-way trust in play
at SAS is the company's remarkable commitment to employee blogs:
according to the employment site SnagAJob.com, it sponsors over 700
of them!

For SAS, trust in employees is nonnegotiable. It's also a sound business investment. In an industry where 22% annual turnover rates are
common, SAS's is consistently below *one-fifth* of that, less than 4%. It's
not the perks alone that make figures like that possible; it's management's ability to hire trustworthy people and then to step back and
prove (not just say) that the team members are in fact trusted. Current
estimates of the dollar savings SAS enjoys as a direct result of being
able to trust—and retain—its key employees stand at approximately
$80 million a year. "People stay," Davis says, "and that translates into
a consistent face to the customer. It also translates into quality of the
software because you're not spending a lot of time hiring, training,
and retraining."[16]

Ultimately, Davis observes, "we're not just selling technology to companies. We are selling a relationship." And relationships are built, first
and foremost, on trust. That goes for employee relationships—and also
for relationships with customers!

Are your employees truly trusted and empowered to do the job they were hired to do?

! ART #41: Once you've hired people you can trust, let them know
you trust them. Don't just say it. Prove it, and people will reward
you with their loyalty.

! ART #42: If you want intense loyalty from your customers, you
must be intensely loyal to your employees.

CELEBRATE!

Amazement Revolutionary: The Scooter Store, Ltd.

Enterprise Focus: Power mobility

Headquarters Location: New Braunfels, TX

Website: www.thescooterstore.com

What You Need to Know: A leading producer of power wheelchairs and scooters. Founded in 1991, the Scooter Store currently has more than 2,000 employees. *Fortune* magazine named the company as one of its 100 Best Companies to Work For in 2004 and 2010. The Scooter Store is also a member of the Inc. 500 Hall of Fame.

One of the Scooter Store's six stated core business principles is this refreshingly direct piece of instruction: "have fun." (The other five, in case you're interested, are "always do the right thing," "focus on the customer," "grow aggressively," "achieve financial success," and "be phenomenal."[17] At the Scooter Store, which has received many honors and accolades over the years for both its marketplace achievements and its upbeat organizational culture, people are truly committed to the total workplace engagement that I call Serious FUN.

In support of the "have fun" goal, the Texas-based purveyor of power wheelchairs and scooters, which is 40% employee-owned, keeps a full-time vice president of celebration on staff. This executive oversees dozens of high-energy workplace celebrations over the course of the year. The Scooter Store's gleefully varied workplace looks for excuses to stop work and enjoy full-scale pep rallies, complete with confetti. In fact, the Scooter Store is the largest commercial consumer of confetti in the state of Texas. The "excuses" include celebrations for local sports teams, birthdays, anniversaries, and more. For the company's fifteenth anniversary, they took every employee on a fancy cruise. This company is all about celebration and fun!

You might think that many parties would be a distraction, but the company's CEO, Doug Harrison, would disagree. He holds to the philosophy that the more creative and engaging the celebrations the company sponsors are, the more committed and content Scooter Store employees are likely to be. (Actually, he calls them "employee-owners," not employees.) Harrison may have a point. The firm has a reported 2% annual turnover rate within its call center operations—an astonishingly low figure. It has also grown steadily over the years and is currently a major player in the power wheelchair and scooter sector, selling over $300 million worth of vehicles annually.

All those celebrations help create the team's sense of *fulfillment* on the job. So does the pervasive culture of total engagement on the part of employees and employee-owners. Their *unique* backgrounds, feedback, and ideas drive both team goals and team tactics—and build a wave of positive expectation for the *next* day's activities.

Some of the employee meetings feel more like miniature parties or celebrations. For instance, the typical working day at the Scooter Store begins with a morning huddle for each work team. This fast-paced team discussion lasts roughly fifteen minutes; during that time, individual employees share their own ideas on what the top priority for the day should be and what obstacles stand in the way of fulfilling that priority. A team vote determines the group's first priority for the day, and the results of that vote are briskly forwarded on for review and discussion by another lightning-round huddle, this one attended by company managers. Eventually, all the team priorities reach the senior executive team. On Fridays the pattern changes, and there are freewheeling group encounters centered around a list of agenda items known as IQs—short for issues and questions—that are related to attaining each team's quarterly goals, referred to as "rocks." **Notice the unorthodox terminology: huddles, IQs, rocks. These vocabulary changes are not minor details; they're major strategic decisions that give Scooter Store gatherings a uniquely positive attitude and atmosphere, and give every working day a celebratory feel!**

Working for the Scooter Store is an addictive hybrid of party, high-powered brainstorming session, and hundred-yard dash. Because of the positive workplace atmosphere, employees emerge from their celebrations *locked into* their personal and team objectives. The company's record of growth and profitability supports Harrison's contention that "companies can provide a pleasant workplace for employees, yet still accomplish the business objectives of the company."

> *When was the last time you threw a party in the workplace?*
> *What reasons, both business and personal, does your*
> *organizations have to celebrate?*

! ART #43: Have fun; find lots of reasons to celebrate. Yes, small successes and employee milestones are worth celebrating! A culture of celebration can lead to deep fulfillment, long-term employee retention, and an improved customer experience.

! ART #44: Even companies that sell the most serious products and services have reasons to celebrate.

! ART #45: Change the vocabulary, and you change the attitude and the atmosphere!

RECAP: AMAZEMENT STRATEGY #2—HAVE SERIOUS FUN

To implement this Amazement Strategy, try these ideas:

- Engage your employees in the same way you want them to engage your customers, as Baptist Health South Florida does.
- Use regularly scheduled all-team meetings to energize everyone, connect with everyone, and reinforce your organization's service vision, as Alston & Bird does.
- Consider giving your most creative people the opportunity to

spend at least part of their time on self-directed projects that will also create value for the customer, as Google does.

- Listen to what your employees are saying about work/life balance, as Slalom Consulting does.

- Send employees thank-you notes to celebrate examples of superior service, as Thomas Interior Systems does.

- Win intense loyalty from your customers by first earning intense loyalty from your employees, as SAS does.

- Have fun and find lots of reasons to celebrate, as the Scooter Store does.

- Key point: Your employees come first—because they are the key to generating your customers! If employees are not operating within the cult of amazement, they won't amaze your customers. On the other hand, if your employees *are themselves* amazed, they will make it their business to amaze your customers.

CHAPTER SIX

STRATEGY #3:
CULTIVATE PARTNERSHIP

Organizations that operate within the cult of amazement attempt to create partnerships with their customers. Partnership is when customers think of you as a business partner—as opposed to *just another company they do business with*.

Amazing organizations get customers so accustomed to a superior level of service that customers come to rely on it. Once customers start to think of you as a partner, they begin to exclude your competitors from the equation.

As we learned from American Express, there is a powerful competitive advantage in adopting a strategy of proactive customer engagement. **Proactive** engagement means connecting with the customer in a way that helps to resolve both immediate problems and future problems that the customer hasn't even thought about yet. Doing this *exceeds the customer's expectations*.

Of course, there are many ways to exceed expectations. Yet most organizations don't take advantage of even a fraction of the available opportunities to go above and beyond the call of duty. Exceed expectations once, and you start to create confidence. Exceed expectations consistently, and you can build confidence. Build up enough confidence, and the customer relationship rises to the level of partnership. **This is the level where your customers anticipate and expect amazement.**

In a partnership, customers look forward to a minimum level of service that is consistently and predictably above average. Their confidence in your company is so firm that they forgive the occasional problem, just as we would overlook an occasional glitch in our relationship with a trusted business partner because of our underlying belief that whatever issues arise can be successfully resolved. The customer anticipates the best, not the worst, from organizations that are operating within the cult of amazement.

Note that *you* cannot make the customer a partner. The customer gets to make that decision! In this chapter, you'll get more examples of organizations that have used what I call the partnership principle to win the hearts, minds, and long-term business of their customers.

Only the customer can make the decision to raise the relationship to the level of partnership.

MAKE THE CUSTOMER'S PROBLEM YOUR PROBLEM

Amazement Revolutionary: Contegix

Enterprise Focus: Website hosting

Headquarters Location: St. Louis, MO

Website: www.contegix.com

What You Need to Know: Contegix is a St. Louis-based managed hosting provider with another office in London, England. The company, which was founded in 2001, currently has forty-two employees.

Stephen R. Covey once said, "If you're proactive, you don't have to wait for circumstances or other people to create perspective expanding experiences. You can consciously create your own." He might have been describing the management philosophy of one of my favorite role model companies: Contegix.

Contegix is a small but growing tech company based in St. Louis whose slogan is "Beyond Managed Hosting." It offers co-location and complete management services for commercial clients who have a broad range of hosting, applications, and cloud computing needs. That's a fancy way of saying that Contegix helps companies with their Website and Internet needs. For instance, if you've ever been to Panera—a popular restaurant chain that offers great bread and other foods, a cool "hangout" environment, and free online access so guests can surf the Web while they munch on their lunch—there's a very good chance you were using Contegix's servers as you logged on to Panera's Website.

One weekend, the director of key accounts at Contegix was proactively monitoring the Internet and social media sites for references to Contegix customers. This kind of monitoring is part of the culture at Contegix. Once a client signs up, the people at Contegix want to know exactly what customers, end users, and others are saying about that client's brand. Contegix's director of key accounts noticed a troubling pattern of messages about a major online ticket agency the company had been working with. This agency was handling the ticketing for an important promotion being sponsored by a major national telecom provider. In response to this promotional campaign, thousands upon thousands of people were storming the agency's Website to get free tickets. The Website traffic was simply overwhelming. Even for the highest-traffic event in their history, the agency had never had this many visitors to its Website. The massive number of online visitors was causing the agency's site to jam. Everything was slowing down!

The online trend the key accounts director had picked up on was quickly confirmed via Facebook and other social media channels.

People were complaining, with greater and greater intensity, about the system overload. Clearly, this was a crisis in the making. Now, given the timing—remember, this was a weekend—the question arises: whose problem was this? Most of Contegix's competitors would have considered the online bottleneck to be the client's problem. As a result, they would have waited for Monday to act, or perhaps have waited for a plea for help from the client. There would then have been a discussion about what kind of deal could be arranged to avert the crisis and handle the overflow.

Are you willing to make the customer's problem your problem?

But that's not what Contegix did. Contegix made the client's problem *their* problem. They reached out and learned that the decision maker who could approve a server upgrade wasn't at work and couldn't be reached immediately. Guess what? It was still Contegix's problem! Contegix—which at the time boasted all of thirty-five employees—promises its clients a 24/7, "we never sleep" business model. It also promises clients a proactive approach to system problems whenever and however they arise. That weekend, Contegix delivered on both promises.

Acting on his own initiative, the director of key accounts launched the process of fixing the problem for the client. The Contegix engineers began putting in extra time and upgrading the equipment to keep their client's system up and running. This decision was breathtakingly simple: give them what we know they want and need, and we'll worry about paperwork later! That weekend, Contegix vowed to give the client as much as they could, even though the engineers initially didn't have any idea how much the fix would cost. Contegix went ahead and installed the additional servers that kept the company's site functioning—and kept the ticket agency's customers happy. As a result, there were no major access problems, the site stayed up, and the agency was able to handle the demand for that extremely important event.

Now, you might think that that's the end of this story, but in fact it's only the beginning. Contegix's senior management reached out to their colleagues at the ticket agency and passed along the following message: "The emergency has passed; you kept all your customers happy, and that makes us happy. You've now got a bank of new servers. You have two options. You can keep them and pay for them or have us come by and pick them up. Either way, there will be no charge for the installation, or for the engineering that was necessary to get you past this crisis."

You read that right: Contegix did not charge for the weekend rush installation that averted the crisis! The stunned customer opted to hold on to the servers; and Contegix turned a casual customer into a long-term business partner. They did that by exceeding expectations! This was not a one-time improvisation, but a conscious choice based on the company's long-term business strategy. Contegix never wants clients to feel like they are being overcharged or sold more equipment than they actually need. That's not the way partners treat each other! According to Contegix CEO Matthew Porter, "Our core value is to wow every customer, on every engagement, with complete integrity—no exceptions."[1]

How could you build up and support an internal standard of exceeding (not just meeting) customer expectations?

! ART #46: When you spot a customer who's in crisis (or about to be), take the initiative to resolve the crisis or alert the customer to the crisis before the customer comes to you.

! ART #47: Make it your organization's goal to amaze every customer, on every engagement, with complete integrity—no exceptions. Once you begin working toward this goal, you will create opportunities to win much deeper business relationships and support new partnerships. Remember: It's all about taking care of the customer!

! **ART #48**: Make the customer's problem your problem.

MAKE IT PERSONAL

Amazement Revolutionary: Ace Hardware Corporation
Enterprise Focus: Retail hardware cooperative
Headquarters Location: Oak Brook, IL
Website: www.acehardware.com
What You Need to Know: Founded in 1924, the firm is owned by the network of Ace retailers. As of 2008, Ace Hardware employs over 100,000 people.

"Part" is the first half of the word "partner." That fact serves as a potent reminder about what we're really trying to do whenever we spot an opportunity to establish partner relationships with our customers: **we're trying to use the spirit of great service to become *part* of their lives.** A true story from the aisles of an Ace Hardware store shows one memorable way this can be done.

An elderly lady was visiting the Ace Hardware Store in Dunedin, Florida, looking at Christmas trees around holiday time. Out in front of the store where the trees were lined up the store manager, Jeffrey Gawel, was helping her to evaluate her choices. She spotted one tree she particularly liked and said to Jeffrey, "Boy, I'd sure love that tree, and I know it would look great in my living room, but it's just too darned tall for me to decorate at my age. I'm not going to make my way up a ladder anymore; I'm too old for that." The woman was simply sharing her thoughts out loud. She certainly wasn't lobbying the manager for his help! So you can imagine her surprise when the manager said, "Oh, that's no problem at all. I'll be happy to deliver to your home, and even help you decorate it."

Surely he was kidding!

But he wasn't kidding, not by a long shot. For the next *nine years* this store manager honored a tradition he himself created: the tradition of putting up this elderly customer's Christmas tree and decorating it for her, with all the cherished family mementos she had stored in her Christmas boxes. She had a lot of ornaments her mother and sisters had made for her over the years. Every year he heard the same stories, but he always enjoyed them. He says it was like spending time with a new grandma. She gave him a piece of banana bread and a Diet Coke every time! Jeffrey only stopped the tree-trimming tradition when his friend finally passed away in her eighties. There were only ten people at her funeral. He was one of them.

She had told her neighbors all about Jeffrey and the wonderful thing he had done. As a result, many of them came in to shop at his Ace Hardware store. This manager became much, much more than a hardware store manager for that customer when he offered to set up her tree. He became a member of the family. He became part of her *life*!

What personal connection can you make to take your relationship with a customer to a deeper level?

! ART #49: Look beyond business for a way to connect with your customer at a deeper, personal level. Doing this can help you create both evangelism and intense, unshakeable loyalty.

CONSISTENCY CREATES CONFIDENCE

Amazement Revolutionary: Lenny's Sub Shop
Enterprise Focus: Franchise restaurant chain

Headquarters Location: Memphis, TN

Website: www.lennys.com

What You Need to Know: Founded in 1988, the chain has approximately 200 franchises in twenty states.

Some people misunderstand what I'm getting at when I talk about creating amazing partnerships with customers. That's because there's something quite unexpected about these amazement-level partnerships, something that goes back to the partnership principle I mentioned earlier: Partnership, in a service context, is not about you turning the customer into *your* strategic partner, although that may happen from time to time. It's about being so good the customer makes you *their* partner by coming to count on you.

Remember: it's the customer's decision, not yours!

Your goal is to deliver a level of amazement that leaves people wanting to deepen the relationship. Let's look at a perfect example of a truly powerful partnership that develops because of one thing: confidence. This is about creating amazement over and over again. The customer owns the experience and expects it, which is why they view the relationship with you and/or your company as something more than just a relationship with a vendor or supplier. This example of partnership comes from simply providing great customer service, a *predictably* positive experience that the customer can count on and therefore *own*.

This role model comes from an industry where a lot of people would *not* expect to hear the word partnership: the fast food industry, or as the insiders prefer to describe themselves, "the quick serve" industry. Lenny's Sub Shops is a Memphis-based national chain whose relentless emphasis on generous servings, high value, and superior service has gotten other national quick-serve chains to take notice. Lenny's delivers such exceptional service that restaurant industry experts describe them as crossing over into the higher-level service category of casual dining!

In case you're wondering what partnership could possibly look like in the context of a restaurant chain that serves submarine sandwiches, here's your answer, in the form of a testimonial from a loyal customer referencing one of Lenny's airport locations:

> *Unlike [the experience at] every other airport dining establishment, I wasn't given a heap of sass from the staff [at the Memphis airport's Lenny's Sub Shop]. Even at 9 a.m., the staff was friendly and ready to make cheese steaks, even cracking some jokes. This Lenny's is how things should be done, and I'm already excited to drive an hour to the Fredricksburg, V.A. location ASAP!*[2]

This may sound like just plain old-fashioned good service, but hear me out; I'm about to prove to you that Lenny's really has risen to the level of partnership with some of their guests. This particular example is partnership at the level of amazement. Notice that the customer has come to *count on* the high level of quality and service received. In other words, in keeping with the true definition of amazement, Lenny's is delivering a consistent, predictably above-average (or better) experience.

Other unsolicited customer testimonials about this specific airport location tell how guests plan to bring others in to experience Lenny's great subs—and how some people even plan their flight layovers around mealtimes, so they can take full advantage of the now-legendary Lenny's outlet at Gate B4 of the Memphis airport!

What on earth generates this kind of buzz, this kind of devotion? It starts with great food, of course. Lenny's regular-size subs are about seven-and-a-half inches long, boasting half a pound of meat and cheese; large-size subs are fifteen inches long with about a pound of meat and cheese. The chain's cheesesteaks and other sandwiches have certainly developed a passionate constituency of advocates. But that isn't *all* that motivates someone to patronize Lenny's. The great food is only the beginning. Lenny's army of evangelists, including the one I quoted above, have something very interesting in common. They typically praise the *staff* as often as they do the food!

So what are those front-line people doing that is creating these customer/guest accolades? They are emphasizing the Lenny's *personality*! George Alvord, the CEO of Lenny's, has made the concept of *personality* central to his franchise operation. He tells everyone that the personality of a Lenny's store is just as important as the food. It is the combination of over-the-top service mixed with the outgoing personalities of the restaurant's employees that makes the company successful and creates true partnership.

Consider the following examples of store personality, all of which deliver a consistent, predictably above-average service experience to Lenny's patrons.

- One franchise owner told me she has trained staff to recognize repeat customers who make a habit of ordering exactly the same sub, time after time. Whenever a counter person spots such a customer walking through the door, the team gets to work making that customer's favorite sub *before the order is placed*. It's usually ready by the time the customer reaches the cash register. Would that put a smile on your face? I know I'd remember that level of service and come to count on it!

- Another franchise owner told me he had a special procedure in place for rainy days. When it's raining, and a Lenny's employee spots a customer heading for the entrance to the restaurant, the team member rushes out to the parking lot *with an umbrella* to walk the guest into the store!

- Yet another team lightens the mood by yelling out the words "SUB SHOP!" when a new customer walks in the establishment. Try to forget that!

Thanks to a dedicated franchise network that operates within the cult of amazement, Lenny's customers have come to expect superior-quality food and a positive emotional experience from the chain. They make a habit of coming back for more of both!

What operational consistencies will create customer confidence in your organization?

! ART #50: Create confidence. Deliver service that's consistent and so good that customers make you their partner because they can count on you, without fail, every time.

! ART #51: Identify and recognize repeat customers. Make them feel special and amaze them.

GO THE EXTRA MILE

Amazement Revolutionary: Ibrahim's Auto Shop
Enterprise Focus: Auto repair
Headquarters Location: Worcester, MA
What You Need to Know: This solo entrepreneur's business serves a small but devoted following of customers in Central Massachusetts.

I asked a friend of mine who lives in Massachusetts to think of a product or service provider he had come to count on and wouldn't stop working with under any circumstances—even if he happened to get a significantly lower price somewhere else.

He instantly answered, "Ibrahim."

I said, "Who's Ibrahim?"

He said, "Ibrahim's my mechanic. And he's going to *stay* my mechanic!"

How did Ibrahim—who cultivates a group of dedicated, price-*insensitive* repeat clients like my friend—win this level of partnership? It turns out that he makes a point of doing three things that instantly stand out in his customers' minds, three things they quickly come to rely on.

1. He goes to the customer. When someone has car trouble, that person is often (surprise, surprise) without transportation. What do some auto service shops say when you call and tell them about a problem you're having? Bring it in to the shop. (Translation: Pay us, or someone else, to tow it into the shop.) Ibrahim's response is, "I'll be right over." He will troubleshoot and diagnose your car's problem on the spot and, if humanly possible, fix it on the spot.

2. He tells the truth. Not a radical concept, but it is nevertheless a competitive differentiator in this particular service field, and in many others as well. Ibrahim never, ever misleads a customer about the nature of a problem or about how much in the way of time, parts, and/or outside help it will take him to fix it. If the problem you're asking him to resolve is truly minor in nature (such as an electrical problem that requires replacing a blown fuse), he fixes your car for free!

3. He provides what he estimates, plus a little extra at no cost. My friend was having a leaky sixteen-year-old radiator replaced. Ibrahim noticed the engine was low on oil and topped it off at no extra charge. These little extras always seem to sneak into the jobs he estimates. Most mechanics spend a fair amount of time explaining why the bill is *higher* than the quote. Ibrahim ends up explaining why he did *more* than he quoted for—without charging anything additional. That's going the extra mile!

Some might call the above good service, and they would be right. These three simple steps are also common sense. Yet somehow they're pretty uncommon in the world of auto repair. Other auto mechanics in Ibrahim's home town generally *don't* do these three things—and don't create a level of confidence that rises to the level of partnership.

What's your equivalent of "the extra mile"?

! ART #52: Identify what customers like least about your industry. (The problems you uncover might not necessarily be about you and your company.) Work to eliminate any and all of these customer preconceptions.

! **ART #53**: If doing so can fit into your business model, go to the customer (instead of making him or her come to you).

! **ART #54**: Give a little more than the customer thinks you are going to give. Little extras you don't charge for can go a long way!

! **ART #55**: Amazing levels of service can help make price less relevant.

DO WHAT YOU SAY YOU'LL DO

Amazement Revolutionary: Quick Transportation
Enterprise Focus: Transportation
Headquarters Location: Orlando, FL
Website: www.quicktransportation.com
What You Need to Know: One of Orlando's premier ground transportation companies, Quick Transportation has thirty-three vehicles including taxi-cabs, vans, and sedans. The company's goal is to "provide the highest quality transportation, at the best value, while ensuring the complete satisfaction of each and customer."[3]

One of the simplest and most effective ways to make customers feel confident enough in what you do to make you their partner is simply to **do what people are counting on you to do—not just once, not just twice, but every single time.**

Let me give you an example of how this plays out in my world. As a professional speaker, I travel a lot. As a matter of fact, over the course of a year, I leave my home town of St. Louis by air an average of once a week. Over the years, I've paid for a lot of rides to and from a lot of airports. If you have read any of my other books, you may remember me writing about Frank, the taxicab driver from Dallas, Texas, who delivers amazing service. Frank has since retired, and my new champion in the arena of ground transportation is Al Castagna, owner of Orlando's Quick Transportation.

About fifteen years ago, I happened to hop into a cab that Al was driving, and I was impressed by his personal attention to me as a customer. Fast-forward to my last trip to Orlando, which was just a few months ago. Even though Al now owns a fleet of cars and employs a staff of drivers, he still makes a point of picking me up personally and getting me where I need to go. Over the course of all those years, Al has never, ever been late. Not once. He has always been there waiting for me, every time I walk out of the Orlando airport.

Of course, Al is a pleasant fellow who delivers great service, which helps. What I want you to notice, though, is that by consistently meeting my expected and basic standard of simply showing up on time, Al has earned my complete confidence, to the point that I would not ever consider hiring anyone else to take me to and from the airport in Orlando. As a result, Al has become my transportation partner.

What do your customers count on you to deliver?

! ART #56: Sometimes, all you have to do is what people would expect you to do. The ability to consistently meet a certain minimum expected standard can give you and your organization a massive competitive advantage.

! ART #57: Be on time, every time. No exceptions.

CREATE A CUSTOMER SUPPORT NETWORK

Amazement Revolutionary: Jeffrey Silverstone (Wells Fargo Advisors)
Enterprise Focus: Financial services
Headquarters Location: St. Louis, MO

Website: https://home.wellsfargoadvisors.com/jeffrey.d.silverstone
What You Need to Know: Wells Fargo Advisors is one of the nation's premier financial services firms, with a network of nearly 16,000 financial advisors.

Jeff Silverstone, my financial advisor for the last twenty-five years, works with Wells Fargo Advisors. He sells stocks, bonds, and mutual funds; however, he wants his clients to view him as a financial advisor involved in *all* things financial—not *just* stocks, bonds, and mutual funds. For example, if I have questions about certain financial issues (such as estate planning, real estate, or accounting) that extend well beyond Jeff's product line and his formal areas of expertise, he still wants me to call him.

And I do. I wouldn't make major decisions in *any* of those areas without first hearing Jeff's recommendation. That's because I've come to rely on Jeff as a critical conduit of financial expertise. I know that, even if my requests for advice fall outside his own personal areas of expertise, he has a team of experts he consults with who can help me. These are people who know their stuff! I'm confident that Jeff will leverage the considerable power of his Rolodex to get me the answers I need and guide me in making the right decisions.

This special kind of relationship—the one where Jeff serves not only as my stockbroker, but as my trusted advisor in all financial matters—didn't happen simply because I like Jeff as a person. It happened because he has built credibility and confidence into our relationship. He did this with his own expertise, of course, but he also combined that expertise with the knowledge and experience of his own personal network of experts.

How can you use your network of personal and professional allies for the benefit of your customers?

! **ART #58**: Knowledge can create credibility and confidence, which are essential ingredients in any partnership relationship.

! ART #59: Being a trusted advisor doesn't always mean having all the answers. It means knowing where to get the answers and knowing how to use the information you uncover on someone else's behalf.

ALIGN ON THE BRAND PROMISE

Amazement Revolutionary: FedEx
Enterprise Focus: Courier/shipping
Headquarters Location: Memphis, TN
Website: www.fedex.com
What You Need to Know: A global leader in transport, shipping, logistics, and workplace support. The company was incorporated in 1971 and began operations in 1973; it employs over 280,000 people.

FedEx—the courier and shipping giant previously known as Federal Express—remains the beneficiary of one of the most memorable and enduring brand promises in the history of American commerce: "When it absolutely, positively has to be there overnight." As a shipping and courier customer who considers FedEx a partner, I can personally attest to the power of that promise. Even today, when overnight shipping represents only one of several lines of business that the company operates, the FedEx brand promise remains virtually impossible to forget. And here's where I'm going to surprise you: I can personally attest to the fact that FedEx *does not always manage to keep that promise.* Yet I still think of them as a partner!

As anyone who ships a great deal with this company over a long period of time can confirm, every once in a while something *does* go wrong with a FedEx shipment: the package gets lost or it doesn't show up on time or some other issue arises. **On those rare occasions when there is a problem, a customer can expect positive interaction and support from**

FedEx. This interaction is more than a matter of FedEx employees being nice on the phone. They are *personally committed* to fulfilling the FedEx brand promise.

That's called organizational alignment, and it's a consistent hallmark of a company that has gotten its people to engage in, connect with, and live by a service mantra that supports the brand promise that the customer hears. The organization's alignment on the FedEx brand promise is the reason so many companies consider FedEx their partner when it comes to shipping.

*What is your organization's promise to its customers—
and is your team aligned on it?*

! ART #60: Create a brand promise that is so strong and so compelling that it makes your customers want to become your partner.

! ART #61: Align your team on the brand promise so they understand it even better than your customers do. They must live it, breathe it, and deliver it.

RECAP: AMAZEMENT STRATEGY #3—CULTIVATE PARTNERSHIP

To implement this Amazement Strategy, try these ideas:

*   Make the customer's problem your problem, as Contegix does.
*   Look for ways to connect with your customer on a personal level, as the manager at the Ace Hardware store did when he helped an elderly customer trim her Christmas tree.
*   Use your organization's *personality* to deliver a consistent, predicable experience of above-average service, as Lenny's does. The key is to make experience predictable, which is what creates confidence.

- Look for opportunities to give a little more than the customer expects, as Ibrahim does. A minor investment in going the extra mile can have a major impact on customer loyalty.
- Be on time, every time, without exception, as Quick Transportation does. This strategy is about doing what you say you will do—every time.
- Use knowledge and your own network of expert advisors to create credibility and confidence (essential ingredients in a partnership relationship), as Jeff Silverstone at Wells Fargo Advisors does.
- Align the team on your organization's brand promise, as FedEx does. That means your employees understand it better then your customers do. Your employees must live it, breathe it, and deliver it.
- Key point: If the customer relies upon you and only you, has confidence in you, and expects that any problems that arise will be resolved successfully, you have entered the realm of partnership.

CHAPTER SEVEN

STRATEGY #4:
HIRE RIGHT

**Companies that operate within the cult of amazement hire for
attitude first, then train for skills.**

Y ou may have already heard someone, somewhere, advocate on behalf
of the principle that to build a great customer-focused organization,
you must *hire for the attitude, then train for the skill*. I buy into this principle. In this chapter, you will find evidence of the power of this powerful
human resource idea.

Of course, this principle does *not* mean that skills don't matter in
the hiring process! For example, if you're hiring nurses, you will need
someone with a degree in nursing to fill the open position; no amount
of attitude will compensate for that skill gap! It's just as important to
remember, however, that some applicants who *do* have nursing degrees
will present attitudes that turn out not to be a good fit for your organization. If you are committed to launching an Amazement Revolution,

then you have an obligation to identify the applicants who present both the background *and* the outlook you are searching for.

With that much said, it's worth noting here that there are some prominent companies—American Express and Zappos among them—who have made the strategic decision to opt for *less* technical knowledge in favor of *more* service orientation and "people skills" in their front-line customer service hires. You'll recall that American Express made a conscious choice to recruit from the hospitality industry rather than the credit card field, and they also chose to play down some of the technical aspects of their own internal training in order to boost the "soft skills" quotient of their service professionals. These decisions de-emphasized the technical side and emphasized the people skills side of the equation.

However you go about establishing the right balance between specialized knowledge and "soft skills," you should know that truly amazing companies always try to hire for the right cultural fit when it comes to recruiting staff. These companies recruit candidates who have the kind of attitude that can eventually turn them into service superstars. *Just* having the skills—*just* knowing what buttons to push—is not enough! The new hire must be able to align with the mission, which is to amaze customers.

Although I speak often on the topic of hiring as it affects the field of customer service, I realized as I was working on this chapter that it would benefit from some in-depth experience from an expert in the field. So I contacted my friend Mel Kleiman, president of Humetrics, a global leader in helping companies recruit, select, and retain great employees. He agreed with my approach to this chapter and shared some interesting tips and strategies to spot the best customer service candidates.

Mel suggested that an employer ask a single question during an interview that effectively spotlights *both* attitude and skills. For instance, a chain of beauty salons asks its applicants for stylist positions, "How much did you pay for your shears?" A higher dollar figure might indicate that the applicant has more pride in his or her work, and it may even indicate a higher skill level. Mel also shared another excellent technique from one of his clients and encouraged me to use it in this book. As a result, the Midwestern super-market chain Hy-Vee became one of this chapter's role models.

The very first role model I want to share with you comes from my own personal list of favorites in the realm of amazing hiring strategies. Its innovative hiring practices inspired this entire chapter!

AUDITION FOR ATTITUDE

Amazement Revolutionary: The Fudgery

Enterprise Focus: Retail fudge stores

Headquarters Location: Gainesville, GA

Website: www.fudgeryfudge.com

What You Need to Know: The Fudgery, known as "Fudgemakers to America," was founded in 1980 and now has twenty-nine locations throughout the United States.

"Here's your chance to sing, dance, or use your own special personality to be the center of attention, while making fudge, friends, and money!"

That's what prospective job seekers see when they visit the Website of the Fudgery, self-proclaimed "Fudgemakers to America." Translation: Don't apply for a front-of-house job if you're shy around other people.

This outfit is not just looking for fudge lovers, but for fudge lovers with a distinctly outgoing personality. That's why the Fudgery has rolled out an innovative, unconventional hiring process, one that often bewilders applicants who expect a standard-issue job interview. If you want to make fudge at the Fudgery, you should expect the unexpected—not just an interview, an audition. Expect to be asked to *sing for your job*! The job description to prospective employees continues:

The Fudgery is now auditioning/accepting applications for a cast of enthusiastic, outgoing, hardworking characters for all of our locations. We have retail management and entry-level retail positions available with competitive salaries and benefits. The Fudgery promotes from within and is a great company to build a career or work for the summer. We even have housing available at Myrtle Beach for employees who seek to spend the summer at the beach working for America's favorite fudge stores.

Did you notice that job description did not contain one word about the importance of possessing fudge-making skills? The Fudgery can teach you how to make fudge. What they can't teach you, however, is the proper attitude, personality, and outlook. You have to bring that much to the interview.

Who runs a chain of fudge stores this way? The man who coined the phrase "interactive retail," that's who. His name is A. C. Marshall, and he knows exactly what kinds of people he wants to see dealing with customers: unapologetic extroverts who live for a chance to step into the spotlight. Why *shouldn't* he ask people to sing during the job interview? After all, they're not just selling fudge—they're selling interaction. And at the Fudgery, even the customers get to do a little singing!

Back in 1980, when Marshall opened his first store in North Carolina, he insisted on a floor plan that gave him, the fudge maker, the opportunity to get plenty of face time with all the fudge lovers who stepped into his place of business. Marshall whistled for them, told them jokes, and sang for them as he made fudge, turning what might have been a simple visit to a sweet shop into an impossible-to-forget serving of culinary performance art.

The Fudgery calls the form of retail that Marshall pioneered "fudge in the round." Three decades later, he's managed to recreate the excitement in over thirty stores across the country by recruiting and evangelizing a band of fudge-loving amateur entertainers. If you make the cut at auditions, it's because Marshall and his team know you are willing to buy into the Fudgery's fun-loving culture.

That culture is epitomized by the company's carefully crafted customer experience, which is defined as follows:

You've only been to the Fudgery if...
You detected the aroma of fudge boiling in a copper kettle;
You saw a cast member delight an audience with song, dance, and jokes;
You heard, "You've got to sing for your fudge";
You indulge in the taste of fudge still warm from its meticulous batching
and cooking and skilled crafting into a mouth watering scrumptious loaf;
You raise your right hand and say, "I... (your name)... promise to always
LOVE THAT FUDGE!"[1]

This is the level of amazement the Fudgery wants their customers to experience. Knowing how to make good fudge *is not enough* to deliver that experience! Performance skills are an important part of the equation. Knowing that, Marshall utilizes a recruiting and hiring process that is built around the idea that the prospective employee must "sing for the job"! The Fudgery's hiring process weeds out the potential true believers and the true *performers* from the rest of the pack. That's the goal of any audition, after all: to identify the people who are capable of delivering the very best performance.

What one question or request can you ask in an interview that will immediately tell you whether the applicant matches your culture—and is capable of amazing your customers?

! **ART #62**: Hire for attitude first, skills second.

! **ART #63**: Don't be afraid to use an unconventional hiring process, such as an audition, to identify the best personality fit for the job.

! **ART #64**: Use the interview process to figure out whether the applicant will best fit into your culture.

HIRE FOR PASSION

Amazement Revolutionary: New Chapter, Inc.

Enterprise Focus: Organic vitamin and food supplement producer

Headquarters Location: Brattleboro, VT

Website: www.newchapter.com

What You Need to Know: Founded in 1982, the company produces and sells a wide range of organic vitamins and nutritional supplements. Its trademarked slogan is "The Whole Truth."

Tom Newmark is a man on a mission. And he's got an army of true believers who are passionate in support of that mission.

The CEO of New Chapter leads one of the nation's leading organic vitamin and supplement companies. I asked him how he achieved success, and he told me one of his "secrets": wherever possible, replace outsiders from traditional sales and distribution channels with members of your internal community of employee evangelists.

Several years ago, New Chapter relied on outside distributors to sell their products in retail outlets. This traditional way of getting the products sold just wasn't working. The salespeople working with the distributors weren't fulfilling the brand's potential. They weren't emotionally connected to New Chapter's commitment to organic processes, sustainability, and social responsibility. But New Chapter's employees were. So he turned them into salespeople!

Revenue skyrocketed. Tom is quick to point out, though, that his strategy will only work when the employees are in full alignment with the organization's mission and values. In New Chapter's case, those values are as follows:

We believe the natural purity of organic ingredients is better for people.
We believe organically grown ingredients are better for the environment.
We believe organic, biodynamic farming helps to protect our world for future generations.[2]

Not all vitamin and supplement companies buy into those values. Yet as a result of maintaining those values, Newmark has attracted a certain type of employee—and a certain type of customer. "True believers" have become Tom's best salespeople because of the strong values they share with the organization and its customers. The fact that most of them had no formal sales experience turned out to be irrelevant.

New Chapter proves the point yet again: hire for attitude first and skills second!

What values and/or beliefs does your organization share with its best employees—and its best customers?

! **ART #65**: In the recruiting, hiring, and retention process, look for the "true believers" of your product, philosophy, mission, and values. Whether or not they have formal sales experience, these people can become your best sales force.

! **ART #66**: At the very best companies to work for, employees don't just "show up for work"—they evangelize on behalf of the organization.

DEFINE "SERVICE"

Amazement Revolutionary: Nordstrom, Inc.
Enterprise Focus: Upscale department store chain
Headquarters Location: Seattle, WA
Website: www.nordstrom.com
What You Need to Know: Founded in 1901, Nordstrom currently operates 112 department store outlets and employs 52,000 people. A leader in the service world for decades, the firm is one of the most honored retailers in American history, and has been

named multiple times to *Fortune* magazine's 100 Best Companies to Work For list.

Nordstrom, the world-famous department store, *became* world famous because of the customer service reputation the company has generated for more than a century. At the root of this legacy of service is Nordstrom's own version of the familiar Golden Rule, "Do unto others as you would have others do unto you." Nordstrom's twist on this philosophy can be summarized as follows:

> *The Golden Rule*
> *Always think: How will it affect my customer? If I were in the customer's shoes, how would I feel? Do what's right for the customer—and you have done what's right for the organization.*[3]

This simple philosophy, when followed in the real world by employees who understand it, buy into it, internalize it, and then live by it, has led to some truly remarkable interactions with customers. There are many stories about Nordstrom's devotion to service, but probably the most famous is the one about the customer who visited a Nordstrom outlet and demanded a refund on a set of tires he had purchased. The store clerk explained that Nordstrom didn't carry tires and so couldn't have sold the customer the tire. The customer persisted, however, and told the clerk he was positive that he had purchased the tire in that very location.

As it turned out, he *had* bought the tire at that location—before Nordstrom opened a store there. The space had previously housed a tire retailer. The clerk studied the receipt, thought for a moment—*and then processed the refund!* Whether or not the clerk was right or wrong is not an issue I want to debate. What is more important is that this clerk was making his own best effort to put Nordstrom's version of the Golden Rule into action!

I mention this story in the context of hiring because Nordstrom is always on the lookout for people who *already* look at customer service from this passionate (but generally quite uncommon) point of view. That's why many of Nordstrom's hiring managers ask this simple yet critically important question during job interviews:

What's your definition of customer service?

If the response that comes back is in harmony with Nordstrom's version of the Golden Rule, there's probably a reason to keep talking. If the applicant's personal definition of customer service is out of sync with that concept, then the interviewer knows the candidate likely isn't a good match for Nordstrom's culture.

> ***If you asked a job applicant to define customer service, would it match up with your organization's definition?***

! **ART #67**: Define what customer service means to you and your organization. During the job interview, ask candidates to give you their definition of customer service, so you can see how well their definition aligns with your organization's.

CREATE AN INTERNAL EMPLOYEE REFERRAL PROGRAM

Amazement Revolutionary: Trader Joe's Company
Enterprise Focus: Specialty retail grocery chain
Headquarters Location: Monrovia, CA
Website: www.traderjoes.com
What You Need to Know: Founded in 1958, Trader Joe's now operates 345 stores in twenty-five states. In 2009, *Consumer Reports* magazine named the chain as one of the two best supermarket chains in the nation.[4]

Trader Joe's, the California-based grocery store chain, offers a selection of eclectic, organic, and gourmet food and beverage items, 80% of which bear the Trader Joe's private label. The chain is legendary for its innovative business model and its commitment to customers. How many grocery store chains have staff members dress up in Hawaiian shirts or offer no-questions-asked refunds?

I was intrigued to learn that Trader Joe's also operates a world-class employee referral program. Just as communities of customers evangelize on behalf of Trader Joe's to introduce friends and family to the experience of shopping there, communities of *employees* evangelize to bring in the very best-qualified applicants to work for the company. A substantial amount of the company's interviews and new hires come about as the result of employee referrals. This is no accident. Trader Joe's has secured the services of a top-notch advertising agency to conduct an *internal* public relations campaign designed to encourage its own employees to refer great applicants! (By the way, the campaign won an industry award for the agency.)

Does this mean you have to put an advertising agency on retainer to have a great workforce? Of course not! What it does mean, though, is that you should consider an active communications campaign *of some kind or another*, one that's designed to get your people to refer great job applicants to your company. If you like the Trader Joe's strategy, you could let your team know that you are looking for good people—just like them—and then let them know you appreciate and are willing to appropriately reward leads that turn into new members of your workplace family.

Is asking your own employees to refer potential applicants a viable strategy for your organization?

! **ART #68**: Keep it in the family! Create an internal employee referral program. The best job leads can come from your current employees.

! **ART #69**: If people don't want to recommend your company as a potential employer to their qualified friends and family members, you should find out why not!

HIRE YOUR BEST CUSTOMERS

Amazement Revolutionary: The Container Store, Inc.

Enterprise Focus: Retail chain offering storage solutions for both home and office

Headquarters Location: Dallas, TX

Website: www.containerstore.com

What You Need to Know: Founded in 1978, the Container Store now operates in forty-nine locations and employs more than 4,000 people.

Lots of industry analysts look with astonishment at the Container Store's stellar record for attracting and retaining great staff. That record is evidenced by the firm's long-running and seemingly bulletproof reputation for superior customer service, as well as by its microscopic annual turnover rate of roughly 10% for full-time employees (in an industry that routinely exceeds 70%).[5] It turns out, though, that the "secret" behind the storage-gadget retail chain's remarkable hiring and retention story isn't a secret at all. In fact, it has been the subject of industry news reports for years.

The Container Store targets the Felix Ungers of this world as customers. In case you aren't old enough to remember Felix Unger, he was the irrepressible neatnik in the old 1970s TV show *The Odd Couple* about two New Yorkers—the neat freak Felix Unger and the slob Oscar Madison. The two found themselves roommates after their respective divorces.

Here's a question: who do you think Felix Unger would prefer to have help from in a retail setting like the Container Store? Answer: a fellow neatnik. This dynamic—container fans interacting with fellow container fans—led the founders of the Container Store to a blinding flash of the obvious: *their very best customers could also be their best employee prospects.* The Container Store actively recruits the same neatniks who shop there to work there, selling organization in the form of containers, bins, and other products designed to make life simpler and less cluttered.

By recruiting some of their employees directly from their own devoted universe of repeat customers, the Container Store has managed to instill a sense of loyalty to the mission among the company's container fans—loyalty that translates to a service ethic that has helped the chain post growth rates that make competitors green with envy.

Which of your best customers would also make great employees or at least refer great employees?

!   **ART #70**: Your best new employee just might be one of your customers—or a referral from one of your customers.

HAVE APPLICANTS OBSERVE AND ASK FOR FEEDBACK

Amazement Revolutionary: Hy-Vee, Inc.
Enterprise Focus: Retail grocery chain operating in the Midwest
Headquarters Location: West Des Moines, IA
Website: www.hyvee.com
What You Need to Know: Founded in 1930, Hy-Vee employs over 55,000 people in 228 stores. J.D. Power and Associates recently ranked the company highest in customer satisfaction with supermarket pharmacies in the Midwest.

Hy-Vee is an employee-owned supermarket chain headquartered in West Des Moines, Iowa. It's the largest employer in the state of Iowa and, according to *Forbes* magazine, the forty-eighth-largest private company in the United States. Like a lot of employee-owned operations, this one has some pretty cool ideas about human resources, recruitment, and hiring. In this case, the idea has to do with a major change in the traditional interview procedure.

Most Hy-Vee stores are hybrid retail centers: expanded-service super-markets that include things like coffee shops, delicatessens, bakeries, and pharmacies, right there on the premises. At many of these locations, the hiring manager will take a job applicant into the store environment, ask him or her to simply observe the swirl of events for ten or fifteen minutes, and then begin the job interview. Having watched the multitiered store in action for an extended period, the applicant is likely to face the following questions:

What was working well?
What wasn't?
What, if anything, would you change in what you saw?
How would you change it?

By incorporating an observation session into the job interview and using questions about that during the face-to-face discussion, Hy-Vee finds out a lot more about its applicants than it would using traditional interview techniques. It gets a better sense of how those applicants think, how creative they are, and what their outlook on the customer is likely to be. For a company that promises—and by all accounts actually delivers—"a helpful smile in every aisle," those kinds of insights take on major importance in the hiring process.

The bottom line, of course, depends on customer reactions to the service delivered by the people who actually get hired. Those reactions are strongly positive, judging from these online reviews:

"I love HyVee for their smiles and helpfulness."[6]

"Excellent customer service and selection."[7]

"The checkers are always friendly and helpful. If you've heard of Hy-Vee, you probably know their slogan is 'Where there's a helpful smile in every aisle.' While it's pretty cheesy, there seems to be some truth to it."[8]

"I always find a bargain here, and I am always satisfied with the low prices and friendly service."[9]

When a supermarket chain gets large numbers of people to go out of their way to say good things about the attitude of the front-line people who interact with customers, there's a pretty good chance that chain is doing something right in their hiring process. Hy-Vee certainly is.

Could you incorporate an observation session
into your next interview?

! ART #71: Ask job candidates to observe their potential future working environments. Get their feedback about what's working and what could be improved. You will learn a lot about the applicant and maybe even something about your organization.

ONBOARDING

Amazement Revolutionary: SnagAJob.com
Enterprise Focus: Job search engine focusing exclusively on hourly and part-time jobs
Headquarters Location: Richmond, VA
Website: www.snagajob.com
What You Need to Know: Founded in 2000, SnagAJob.com has approximately 120 employees. The company was named one of the 50 Best Small Companies to Work for in America by the Great Place to Work Institute.

SnagAJob.com has created the largest hourly and part-time job search engine in the United States. Each and every new SnagAJob.com hire gets a personalized handwritten note from CEO Shawn Boyer and a $100 gift card as a welcoming gesture to the company's latest recruit. This is a nice reward for successfully completing the interview process, and it's especially appropriate to the company's in-depth, decade-long connection with the world of interviews, job offers, and retention campaigns.

It's as though all that networking between prospective employees and prospective employers has given the company some deep insights on two critical cultural values that drive employee buy-in from the very earliest stages of the relationship with the employer: communication and gratitude.

In effect, this is the after-experience principle applied to the world of recruitment. The experience is the interview process; the after-experience takes the form of the surprises that come afterwards. As you'll see in chapter 6, the core requirements for an effective after-experience are that it be *unexpected*, *appreciated*, and *memorable*. The note from the CEO and gift card certainly hits all three requirements, and on top of that, it is authentic. What a great way to welcome someone new to the organization!

How can you welcome new employees in a way that is unexpected, memorable, and appreciated to set the tone for a positive, customer-focused service culture?

! **ART #72**: Send new hires a positive and authentic personal message from senior management to welcome them to their new jobs.

! **ART #73**: Apply the after-experience principle to your recruitment and hiring campaign by giving new hires some type of gift. Keep it simple; you don't need to make the gift extravagant. Your gift should add to the welcoming experience and set the tone for how fellow employees, not just customers, are treated.

RECAP: AMAZEMENT STRATEGY #4—HIRE RIGHT

To implement this Amazement Strategy, try these ideas:

- Audition for attitude first, as the Fudgery does.
- Turn your company's most passionate evangelists into salespeople, as New Chapter has.
- Ask job applicants to define customer service, as Nordstrom does.
- Create and support an internal employee referral program, as Trader Joe's does.
- Turn your best customers into your best employees, as the Container Store does.
- Incorporate an observation period into your interview process, as Hy-Vee does.
- Consider applying the after-experience principle to your recruitment and hiring campaign by giving new hires some type of gift, as SnagAJob.com does.

CHAPTER EIGHT

STRATEGY #5:
CREATE A MEMORABLE
AFTER-EXPERIENCE

**Organizations that operate within the cult of amazement create
after-experiences that are unexpected, appreciated, and memorable.**

Do you remember how American Express followed through with me after I purchased theater tickets for my mother? That was a classic example of a tactical maneuver meant to heighten a customer's perceived experience *following* a service interaction: an after-experience. In this case, it was additional customer service that was provided. The after-experience is usually just a very simple gesture, yet it can have a major impact on a customer's memory of the original experience.

It's tempting to define an after-experience as "what we do after the transaction." In fact, though, as you learned in an earlier chapter, "transaction" is not the best word to use as you strive for an ongoing relationship with the customer. You want to get in the habit of using the word "interaction," which is a better way to describe what you are trying to achieve.

All the other Amazement Strategies in this book involve the organization; this one involves the design of the customer experience itself. As I noted above, an after-experience is tactical in nature. You create an effective after-experience when, after a customer's experience with your organization, you follow through to deliver something that the customer considers unexpected, appreciated, and memorable.

As you will learn, there are many different ways to deliver this kind of positive experience. Some of the role model examples of the after-experience are quite simple, others are a bit more extravagant. All of them, however, require that you look beyond a single interaction with the customer and assume responsibility for the larger relationship.

As simplistic as the after-experience concept may at first appear to be, it is an extremely powerful, extremely effective tactic that can help you raise your customers' awareness of the great service you provide.

It's really a shame how often this simple after-experience idea is overlooked, especially when you consider how incredibly cost effective it can be. I hope you will implement *at least one* of the ideas that appear in this section, so you can see for yourself the powerful effect it can have on long-term customer loyalty. Think for just a moment of how much time, effort, energy, and attention your organization invests to win even a single customer who makes a single purchase. What if I told you that by investing a tiny fraction of what it took your organization to *capture* that customer, you could *retain* that customer and dramatically expand his or her lifetime value to your organization? That's the power of the after-experience, and you can begin harnessing it by implementing just one of the ideas you find here!

THE PERFECT GIFT

Amazement Revolutionary: Premiere Speakers Bureau

Enterprise Focus: Speakers' bureau and talent agency

Headquarters Location: Franklin, TN

Website: www.premierespeakers.com

What You Need to Know: One of the most respected speakers' bureaus in the industry, Premiere Speakers Bureau has offices in Calgary, London, Brisbane, and Rio de Janeiro.

Supporting proactive follow-through *after* the interaction with the customer is one of the keys to building a truly service-driven organization. The lesson here is about giving gifts to customers. The question is, what kind of gift? Plenty of companies send trinkets and knick-knacks to their most important customers once a year. Are these after-experiences?

No. The "send a desk calendar in November" approach may be follow-through of a sort, but it doesn't meet the criteria for an amazement-level after-experience. The desk calendar isn't unexpected, and it certainly isn't memorable. Many different companies *also* send desk calendars, so the gift will very likely go completely unappreciated because there is a good chance that it will never be used, or even noticed!

My good friend Brian Lord is a master of the after-experience. He is one of the truly amazing booking agents at Premiere Speakers Bureau, a full-service speakers' bureau and talent agency that prides itself on delivering a high-end experience to clients and to the talent they book. Brian has elevated follow-through to a fine art, and he's one of my favorite role models in this area because the kind of follow-through he delivers is so often unexpected, appreciated, and memorable.

What I really love is Brian's willingness to "think outside the box" to create unique after-experiences that match up with *individual customers.* Here's my favorite example of that. One day, during a face-to-face meeting, Brian noticed a framed *Sports Illustrated* cover on a client's office wall. It turned out this client was a big fan of the St. Louis Cardinals Hall of Famer Lou Brock. After that client's event was successfully completed, Brian delivered a truly amazing after-experience. As a gesture of thanks and appreciation, he sent his client a baseball *signed by Lou Brock*!

This isn't the typical client gift that might go out to two or three hundred people at the end of the year. It is a truly customized, completely personalized, and amazingly thoughtful post-event gift selected for a specific individual.

Brian's thank you gift to his client hit all three requirements for an amazing after-experience. It was totally unexpected, deeply appreciated, and profoundly memorable.

Brian is great at what he does, but I think the after-experience he created here took him to an even higher level of client amazement, a level that helped solidify a relationship that has lasted for years. And it didn't even cost that much; at less than $25, you certainly couldn't call that autographed baseball an expensive gift. In terms of impact on the customer, however, it was a home run!

How would your customers react to a gift that is truly personal, one that shows that you really put some thought into picking it out?

! **ART #74**: Create an after-experience by following through in a way that is unexpected, appreciated, and memorable.

! **ART #75**: A carefully chosen gift or token of appreciation can show that you really care about an individual customer.

!   **ART #76**: The perfect gift doesn't have to be expensive or extravagant. It just needs to be right for the occasion, for your business, and for your customer.

AN UNEXPECTED THANK-YOU NOTE

Amazement Revolutionary: Missouri Baptist Medical Center
Enterprise Focus: Health care
Headquarters Location: St. Louis, MO
Website: www.missouribaptist.org
What You Need to Know: Missouri Baptist Medical Center is a 489-bed hospital that serves the St. Louis area and specializes in cardiac services, obstetrics, orthopedics, and cancer treatment. The center has been on Thomson Reuter's list of the top 100 hospitals in America for the last two consecutive years.

The after-experience principle is all about effective, creative, proactive follow-through, and the classic example of good follow-through in the realm of customer service would have to be the personalized thank-you note. This simple, extremely powerful tool has been used for as long as anyone can remember by salespeople, entrepreneurs, retailers, and others intent on conveying a personal touch to a customer or prospect.

Please understand, though, that the act of writing a customized thank-you note is not enough to set your organization apart and into the cult of amazement. Yet the tactic of consistently sending thank-you notes when you work in an arena where the customer *does not expect to receive such a note* is a great way to support amazement. Let me share my favorite example of this kind of thank-you note.

A few years back, my wife went to Missouri Baptist Medical Center to undergo minor surgery. Everything went fine. Three days later, when my wife was back home, what did we find as we were going through the day's mail? A handwritten thank-you card from Phyllis Austin, director of surgical services, expressing Phyllis's gratitude to my wife for her choice to have the surgery done at Missouri Baptist Medical Center! There were also handwritten greetings on the card from two of the nurses who had helped my wife, as well as wishes for a speedy recovery from some of the other people on the operating room team. This was a pleasant surprise, as we certainly *didn't* expect that level of recognition from a hospital or an operating room team!

This simple, unexpected gesture instantly made a very powerful positive impression with us about Missouri Baptist Medical Center's level of commitment to its patients. (I have to say, though, that we were already quite impressed with the level of care my wife had received.) That thank-you card, which probably took all of five minutes to write and send, told us something important about the hospital's internal operating culture, about the staff's ability and willingness to work together harmoniously, and about their commitment to consistently delivering both high-quality care and above-average service. It was no surprise to learn, as we did recently, that the hospital had made Thomson Reuter's list of the top 100 hospitals in America for the second straight year.

How would your customers feel if you sent them a personal note
thanking them for their business? Would doing so help you to
stand out from the competition?

!   ART #77: In today's fast-paced world, a personalized thank-you note is often unexpected, sometimes memorable, and always appreciated.

ACKNOWLEDGE IMPORTANT MILESTONES

Amazement Revolutionary: Ranoush
Enterprise Focus: Restaurant
Headquarters Location: St. Louis, MO

Website: www.ranoush.com

What You Need to Know: Ranoush, a local St. Louis restaurant, offers dining in the Middle Eastern style that builds "cultural connections between East and West based on food and enjoyment."[1]

Can you find an unexpected, memorable, and appreciated gift that both celebrates and thanks your best customers at particularly important moments in their lives? If you can, you will be able to keep them thinking about you and your business long after they've completed the "transaction" that gave you the opportunity to pass along the gift!

The St. Louis restaurant Ranoush gave me the idea to start looking for after-experiences in the service realm. I had been there four or five times and decided to book a reservation there to celebrate my birthday. My wife and I had a great time that night, and the food and service were marvelous, as expected. As the evening neared its end, Aboud, the owner of the restaurant, walked over and handed me an unopened bottle of wine.

He said, "Mr. Hyken, I just want to wish you a happy birthday. Here's a bottle of our new house wine for you to enjoy when you get home. We haven't even put it on the menu yet. I sure hope you enjoy it."

It was a wonderful moment, but the real payoff came a week or so later, when my wife and I opened the bottle of wine, relived a great experience from a week before, and started thinking about reasons to go back to Ranoush!

> *How can you incorporate a customer's important personal*
> *dates (such as birthdays, anniversaries, and so on)*
> *to create an after-experience?*

! **ART #78**: Recognize and celebrate the big days in your customers' lives, such as birthdays and anniversaries. By the way, this is easier to do than ever before, thanks to social media applications like Facebook that list such dates.

! **ART #79**: Reward your customers with small gifts of appreciation that will reinforce your brand and make people positively reflect on their experience with you.

TAKE ADVANTAGE OF SLOW TIMES

Amazement Revolutionary: The TruGreen Companies, Inc.

Enterprise Focus: Lawn and Landscape Care

Headquarters Location: Memphis, TN

Website: www.trugreen.com

What You Need to Know: TruGreen is a lawn and landscape care firm that was acquired in 1990 by ServiceMaster, Inc., a privately held Fortune 1,000 company. ServiceMaster employs over 30,000 people; it was founded in 1929.

How do you keep customers thinking about your highly seasonal service brand, even in between purchases or when times are slow?

That's what the people at TruGreen, one of the nation's leading lawn care providers for both homes and businesses, asked themselves. The answer they came up with matches the criteria for a powerful after-experience: unexpected, memorable, and appreciated. What the folks at TruGreen in my part of the country (St. Louis, Missouri) realized was that their customers have an off-season, a period when they don't even *think* about seeding and fertilizing the yard. This special period of down time is known to people in the industry as "winter."

TruGreen concluded that the inevitable winter off-season actually presented a great opportunity for them to win or reinforce brand awareness among their customers, so they did something to take advantage of that opportunity. No, they didn't open up a snowplowing business! Instead, they gave their customers free bags of ice melt, compliments of TruGreen—delivered in person!

The gift was unexpected, appreciated, and memorable, especially when it came time for me to renew my lawn contract for the following year. As you've probably already guessed, I signed up again.

How can you get your customers to remember you when they're not actually using your product or service?

! ART #80: A thoughtful, well-chosen, and unexpected contact during slow times or in the off-season can create a memorable after-experience.

BUILD AN AFTER-EXPERIENCE INTO YOUR MARKETING AND PROMOTION

Amazement Revolutionary: California Pizza Kitchen, Inc.
Enterprise Focus: Restaurant chain
Headquarters Location: Los Angeles, CA
Website: www.cpk.com
What You Need to Know: Founded in 1985, California Pizza Kitchen offers casual fine dining, operates over 230 locations, and employs over 14,000 people.

This after-experience idea falls under the category of "creative promotion." That's perfectly appropriate because certain promotions, as blatant or obvious as they might be as an attempt to win new purchases, can also serve as powerful after-experiences that reinforce memories of a positive interaction with your organization.

California Pizza Kitchen did exactly that with a very creative after-experience promotion I recently experienced firsthand. After I finished my meal, which was great, the server surprised me with a sealed envelope containing a special gift that I was told I couldn't open! Inside the envelope, the server informed me, was a thank-you card featuring a guaranteed prize—anything from 10% off my next meal to $25,000 in cash! Here's the fun part: the sealed envelope could only be opened by a manager when I returned to a California Pizza Kitchen restaurant.

What is the main thing people get from an unknown gift that's not to be used until later? Fun! It's a little bit like becoming a kid again, having to wait to open a holiday gift. When you come back to the restaurant, you get to open your present! Yes, I thought about that envelope after I left the restaurant, and yes, I looked for an opportunity to come back.

Put it all together, and you get a person-to-person promotional after-experience, instead of just a promotion. This kind of ritual definitely delivers a post-dining experience that's unexpected, appreciated, and memorable—and highly likely to inspire a return visit. It did in my case!

How can you incorporate an effective promotion
into the after-experience?

! ART #81: Sometimes a creative promotion can also be a great after-experience. For this to happen, the promotion must be appreciated, must make the customer reflect on a recent positive experience, and must create a sense of anticipation.

GET FACE-TO-FACE

Amazement Revolutionary: Townsend Oil & Propane
Enterprise Focus: Heating oil distributor
Headquarters Location: Danvers, MA
Website: www.townsendoil.com
What You Need to Know: Founded in 1931, Townsend Oil provides customers in Eastern Massachusetts and southern New Hampshire with heating oil and propane. The company is a fourth-generation family-owned and operated business.

Townsend Oil, a Massachusetts-based heating oil distributor, doesn't just deliver the oil on time to the homeowners and businesses it serves. It asks for an in-person follow-up appointment after the oil is delivered. Virtually every customer agrees to that appointment. Why? Because the request for the in-person appointment takes the form of a free annual service and preventive maintenance check on the customer's heating equipment!

That free (and necessary) maintenance assessment is Townsend's after-experience. The yearly follow-up visit delivers legitimate value, keeps Townsend on the customer's radar between visits from the oil truck, and effectively protects the company from most competition. That's because most customers are happy to keep working with an outfit that invests time, care, and personal attention, which in this case means giving the customer a value-added after-experience: assessing the equipment, spotting small problems before they become big ones, and suggesting the right preventative maintenance steps.

How can you create an after-experience
with personal follow-up?

! ART #82: After a customer's initial purchase experience, schedule a follow-up meeting, in person or over the phone, that delivers a value-added benefit that distinguishes you from the competition.

FOLLOW-UP CALLS SHOULD CONVEY GRATITUDE

Amazement Revolutionary: Weiss Brentwood Volvo
Enterprise Focus: Auto sales
Headquarters Location: St. Louis, MO
Website: www.weissbrentwoodvolvo.com
What You Need to Know: Founded in 1976, Weiss Brentwood

Volvo has approximately fifty employees and has been named a Volvo Dealer of Excellence twelve times.

Weiss Brentwood Volvo, an auto dealership in St. Louis, makes a point of following up by phone with its customers after every service appointment. That's not particularly amazing in and of itself, but according to my wife, there's something about the way the calls are delivered that sets these conversations apart from the typical robotic follow-up survey calls some businesses make. The call she got from Weiss Brentwood made my wife feel the dealership was genuinely grateful for her business.

The call didn't feel scripted or rushed or one-sided. It was a genuine *conversation*, and although the person from the Volvo dealership was indeed filling in answers to a prewritten customer satisfaction survey, that didn't make it feel like a "survey call." The customer service representative's conversational style was designed to determine whether or not my wife was truly happy with the service she had received.

Such calls from real, live, *concerned* human beings are pretty rare in the average customer's world. When a call like that follows a recent service experience we have had, when it is delivered in a way that communicates authentic concern for how our experience was, when it leaves us feeling that our feelings about the experience really matter, when the call lets us know that another person is actually grateful for our business—then it's more than just a "follow-up call." It's a powerful after-experience.

Are your follow-up calls focused on the survey or the customer?

! ART #83: Use follow-up calls to accomplish two important goals: first, to let your customer know that he or she is appreciated; and second, to find out how you're doing.

!   **ART #84**: When you're finished with your follow-up call, the customer should feel that the call was more about listening to and thanking him or her, and less about gathering information.

RECAP: AMAZEMENT STRATEGY #5—CREATE A MEMORABLE AFTER-EXPERIENCE

To implement this Amazement Strategy, try these ideas:

- Send a truly personal and thoughtful gift, as Premiere Speakers Bureau does.
- Send a personal thank-you note, as Missouri Baptist Medical Center does.
- Use a customer's important personal dates (such as a birthday or anniversary) to create an after-experience, as Ranoush does.
- Make thoughtful, well-chosen, and unexpected contact during slow times or in the off-season, as TruGreen does.
- Incorporate an effective promotion into an after-experience, as California Pizza Kitchen does.
- Schedule a post-purchase meeting that delivers a value-added benefit, as Townsend Oil does.
- Use follow-up calls to let your customers know they're appreciated and find out how you're doing, as Weiss Brentwood Volvo does.
- Key point: Create after-experiences that are unexpected, appreciated, and memorable.

CHAPTER NINE

STRATEGY #6:
BUILD COMMUNITY

Organizations that operate within the cult of amazement support and derive ongoing value from their communities of loyal customers.

You'll recall that American Express connected the compensation of everyone in the service division—from the company's senior executives down to its front-line customer care people—to the answer given by customers to a simple question: would you recommend American Express to a friend?

Tabulating the response to this question is a sound strategic move, one that aligns the enterprise with the voices and desires of its customers. The question, however, does a lot more than that. It *creates communities of evangelists.* Building this question into American Express's corporate DNA means posing it repeatedly and doing whatever is necessary to *get* people to want to recommend American Express to friends and family.

In this way, the company *supports and learns from* large communities of customers who say they are willing to advocate on behalf of the brand.

Every company that operates within the cult of amazement builds, maintains, and supports a community of evangelists. That's not all. Every truly amazing company uses the feedback it receives from the members of its community to help establish and maintain a unique competitive advantage in the marketplace.

In this chapter, you'll read about seven amazing companies who have learned how to nurture, sustain, and listen to their own communities of passionate enthusiasts. As you will see, this is not a matter of inventing an evangelizing community, but rather a matter of communicating effectively with the individual customers who have *already* established a sense of identity and belonging within your brand. If you treat these people with the respect they deserve and interact with them regularly, they will welcome brand new customers on your behalf, indoctrinate those new customers into the intricacies of your offerings, and act as mentors who help resolve the initial questions and problems that follow an initial purchase. These people will also customize, tinker with, and perhaps even improve on your product/service offerings in ways that add equity value to your enterprise. Last but not least, they will manage impressions on behalf of your organization, get your current customers to buy more, and get new prospects to buy from you for the very first time!

All of this is possible if you are willing to listen to your best customers, support them, and respect them!

GET GREAT IDEAS FROM YOUR CUSTOMERS

Amazement Revolutionary: Harley-Davidson, Inc,
Enterprise Focus: Motorcycles, branded merchandise, consumer finance
Headquarters Location: Milwaukee, WI

Website: www.harley-davidson.com

What You Need to Know: The company produces heavyweight (750 cc-plus) motorcycles. One of the pioneers in motorcycle design, manufacturing, and sales, Harley-Davidson was founded in 1903. Today, it employs over 9,000 people.

Harley-Davidson's corporate legacy—and its formula for success—can be summed up in one short sentence: *Listen to the bikers.*

The storied American motorcycle manufacturer was one of only two national motorcycle producers to survive the Great Depression. How did it manage that? By talking to bikers; specifically, by talking to police officers, who were pretty much the only customers in the early 1930s who still ordered Harleys in significant numbers. Faced with a full-scale market meltdown and four straight years of plummeting sales, Harley started to work closely with police departments around the country; the motorcycle manufacturer shared police officers' concern about an epidemic of road fatalities and supported their ideas with a big nationwide traffic safety campaign. The company also shrewdly rebranded its product as "The Police Motorcycle."

The strategy worked. More and more police departments around the country started ordering Harleys. Sales rose for the first time since the stock market crash of 1929. The company had dramatically expanded an existing community of loyal customers, simply by showing them the respect they deserved, listening to them, and giving them what they wanted. Thanks to the wave of police department purchases, Harley rebounded—and the general population started driving Harleys again, too! The company dominated the field when the market for consumer motorcycles finally recovered, and Harley maintained a dominant position in that market for most of the next four decades.

Fast-forward to 1983. Following fourteen years of disastrous inattention to the issue of quality control, Harley-Davidson was close to bankruptcy. Employee morale was at an all-time low. Competitive pressures from Japanese motorcycle companies were more intense than anyone could remember. Customers were alienated, and quite a few of them were downright hostile to the brand they had once worshipped. After seemingly endless rounds of cost cutting (supposedly to keep Harley competitive), recent models were so poorly designed and built that once-loyal customers dismissed them as "Hardly Drivable." Analysts predicted the company's demise.

A new group of owners took over and made a critical strategic decision to listen to the bikers. What the bikers told them to do was pretty simple: Stop trying to keep up with Japanese styling. Go back to the classic bike designs that earlier generations of bikers rode to define themselves as rebels, as nonconformists, as independent-minded bands of freewheelers. Stop cutting corners. And make Harley a lifestyle again, not just a bike.

It worked! Harley's best customers were indeed willing to pay a premium for something their competitors weren't offering: high-quality reinterpretations of Harley's classic bikes. What's really remarkable is that some of the most popular models featured design refinements that came, not from professional designers, but from the community of Harley riders!

Some of the most famous Harley refinements and design elements from the 1960s and 1970s originated from Harley riders themselves.

Once again, the company rebounded with a vengeance because it listened to and looked for ways to support the lifestyle of its most committed customers. Even today, as the company adjusts to another down period in the market and economy, the community of Harley riders are proving once again that customer-focused companies are far better equipped to ride out the tough times than other companies are. Harley riders aren't just buying motorcycles, after all. Like the police officers of the 1930s, they are buying into a certain image of themselves and making a distinctive social statement.

Harley-Davidson is still a vigorous presence in the marketplace and in popular culture. There are a lot of reasons for that, of course, but one of the biggest reasons is the Harley community itself. Harley remains a force to be reckoned with *because the company still listens to the biker*. That strategic choice pays off in countless ways: in Harley riders' commitment to organize and evangelize on behalf of the Harley brand, in their willingness to buy Harley-branded merchandise and even *finance motorcycle purchases* through the company's new branded financial services unit, and in their ability to share both ideas and complaints with the company.

Having made listening to its fanatical customer base an ongoing part of the business plan, Harley has outlasted another economic downturn. The company's willingness to listen to and find new ways to serve its own best customers has made Harley-Davidson one of the true road warriors of American business.

Could you enlist your most engaged customers to supply you with good ideas?

! **ART #85**: Respect your customer base enough to listen to them and learn what's important to them.

! **ART #86**: When times are tough, remember that listening to your community of evangelists is more important than ever.

! **ART #87**: Bring your best customers into your research and development process.

! **ART #88**: Learn as much as you can, as often as you can, about the lifestyle choices your customers associate with your products and services.

BUILD ETHICS INTO YOUR BRAND PROMISE

Amazement Revolutionary: LUSH, Ltd.
Enterprise Focus: Cosmetics
Headquarters Location: Poole, England
Website: www.lush.com
What You Need to Know: The handmade cosmetics manufacturer and retailer was founded by the English husband-and-wife team of Mark and Mo Constantine in 1994. There are now over 600 Lush stores in forty-three countries.

Some people buy Lush soaps and cosmetics *just* because they're truly great personal care products. A big percentage of the UK company's passionate fan base is hooked on the extraordinary quality the company delivers, and those users are quite likely to sing the company's praises, first and foremost, on product quality.

What makes Lush a true community, though, is what happens within a *subgroup* of those hundreds of thousands of people who are hooked on the high quality of the company's products. People within this subgroup know all about how wonderful the soap is, but they evangelize on behalf of the product and buy it as gift for others for a very different reason.

They evangelize on behalf of Lush because Lush products match up with their ethical values. One of Lush's core corporate beliefs reads as follows:

We believe in buying ingredients only from companies that do not commission tests on animals.

Translation: The ingredients in Lush products are cruelty-free, which means that no animals are harmed in the development or manufacture of Lush goods. The company is a major lobbyist on behalf of consumer awareness of animal testing practices, and it supports worldwide animal rights groups.

If you're unfamiliar with Lush products or new to the controversies in this industry, you may be wondering exactly how soaps and cosmetics can make an ethical statement strong enough to inspire intense customer advocacy of the kind I'm talking about. Animal welfare is a very emotional subject for a major segment of the Lush customer base. This topic is *not* a huge motivator for *everybody* who visits Lush stores or buys online, but it certainly is a hot-button issue for some of them.

Here's the point: You don't have to know or care at all about animal rights to fall in love with Lush. If you *do* know and care about that issue, though, and you happen to make a purchase from the Lush product line, then you may well end up evangelizing for the company. For example, you buy Lush products because you appreciate their quality; you then learn about the cruelty-free manufacturing standard; you tell your friends and family about how much you love the products *and* how much you admire the company's cruelty-free standards. Congratulations! You have just joined the Lush subgroup of cause-driven evangelists!

Can you add an ethical element to your brand promise that motivates people do business with you, not just because you are good, but also because of the good things you stand for?

! **ART #89**: Use your brand to make an ethical statement about something that is genuinely important to you, your organization, and a portion (if not all) of your customers.

BUILD YOUR COMMUNITY AROUND A CAUSE

Amazement Revolutionary: Pedro's Planet, Inc.

Enterprise Focus: Office supplies

Headquarters Location: St. Louis, MO

Website: www.pedrosplanet.com

What You Need to Know: An office supply retailer offering recycling services, Pedro's Planet pursues an environmentally responsible business plan: "Our philosophy has always been to care for you and care for the planet." Headquartered in St. Louis, with a satellite office in Denver and forty-two distribution centers, the firm employs approximately twenty full-time people.

As mentioned in the previous role model example, Lush creates a subgroup within its customer base that shares the company's position on the cause of animal welfare, which is of deep importance to *some* of its users. The office supply outlet Pedro's Planet takes a different approach. The *entire* brand promise itself is built around one cause: reducing the negative environmental impact of office products. That's another powerful recipe for community.

If you buy office supplies from Pedro's, there's really only one driving reason for that: you want to reduce your workplace's impact on the environment we all share as citizens of planet Earth. The company's tagline says it all: "Because good planets are hard to find."

Although the company primarily focuses on the St. Louis, Missouri, and Denver, Colorado markets, it enjoys a nationwide fan base through its online store. It has built a community based on the strength of its appealing and cause-centered brand promise, its excellent customer service, and its value-conscious pricing. If environmental issues are important to you, then the odds are good you'll at least consider becoming a member of Pedro's community of evangelists once you find out about what the company stands for.

*Could you build your brand promise around a cause that
defines your target market?*

! **ART #90**: Build or rebuild your business around a cause that
inspires a community of passionate customers.

KEEP IT SIMPLE

Amazement Revolutionary: In-N-Out Burger

Enterprise Focus: Restaurant chain

Headquarters Location: Irvine, CA

Website: www.in-n-out.com

What You Need to Know: Founded in 1948, the privately held
fast-food chain has over 251 locations. Sandelman and Associates
recently reported that In-N-Out Burger, a regional chain, had higher
consumer satisfaction rankings than national fast-food chains. [1]

As I've noted, the presence of a group of passionately devoted customers
is one of the most obvious signs of a company that's operating within
the cult of amazement. Among other vitally important things they do for
an enterprise, these customers take on the personal mission of introduc-
ing the organization to as many new potential "converts" as possible. A
group of truly dedicated fans in love with a truly amazing company can
sometimes take over most, or virtually all, the work that other companies
categorize as marketing!

That's definitely the case with In-N-Out Burger, a chain serving very
high-quality burgers and fries in only four states: California, Nevada,
Arizona, and Utah. If you look in the dictionary under "word-of-mouth
marketing," you might just see a picture of an In-N-Out Burger drive-
through. In fact, if you happen to live in a city or town that has an In-N-
Out Burger and you're not a committed vegetarian, I'd be willing to bet

that you either already *are* a dedicated fan of In-N-Out Burger, or you have recently been approached by someone who desperately wants you to give the chain a try.

At some point, companies with a following as devoted as that of In-N-Out Burger's face an important strategic decision: do they continue to focus on the handful of products/services that originally won the hearts of their dedicated customer base, or do they try to diversify or grow the line? In-N-Out Burger's answer: keep the number of offerings low and the quality high.

The menu at an In-N-Out Burger restaurant is the antithesis of the menu you find at most major national hamburger chains, which constantly test and add menu items. In-N-Out Burger's menu hasn't really changed since they opened their first restaurant in 1948! As one of the restaurant's evangelists wrote in a recent blog post, "In-N-Out has stuck to their guns and kept the same menu that has led to its continued success: burger, fries, and a drink. Simple = Perfection."[2]

Can you simplify your product or service line to focus on what your community of evangelists wants and loves?

! **ART #91**: It is better to be great at one thing than to be average or mediocre at many.

! **ART #92**: Simplify. Focus relentlessly on giving your community of evangelists exactly what it loves.

BRING CUSTOMERS TOGETHER IN COMPANY-SPONSORED FORUMS

Amazement Revolutionary: Amazon.com, Inc.
Enterprise Focus: Retail
Headquarters Location: Seattle, WA
Website: www.amazon.com

What You Need to Know: A global electronic commerce giant, Amazon employs over 26,000 people and is America's largest online retailer. It was founded in 1994.

You may be used to thinking of Amazon as an incredibly user-friendly, astonishingly efficient online retailer. You may have already known that the company started out specializing in books, and now offers about anything else that can be shipped or downloaded, from clothing to cookware, and from Kindles to karaoke tunes. You may even have admired Amazon's uncanny ability to make on-target recommendations for future purchases based on past purchases—or even based on *nonpurchases,* such as searches you conducted that didn't actually result in an order.

What you may not have realized, however, is that Amazon's reading-group blog (accessible via http://www.amazon.com/gp/daily) is one of the Internet's great gathering places. It's called Omnivoracious, and as the name suggests, it is an online hangout for people who want to discuss just about any subject. Here, Amazon's customers from far-flung corners of the globe congregate virtually to share questions, insights, and obsessions about thousands of subjects, each of which connects indirectly to something that's available for purchase on Amazon's Website. (Book publishers also get involved by cosponsoring some of the content.) These are company-sponsored *discussion groups,* not user groups focused on how to use a specific product or service. (The importance of that distinction will become clear when we look at our next role model, Apple.)

The Omnivoracious network features discussion groups for car enthusiasts, music lovers, culinary devotees, environmentally conscious consumers, and people who feel like sounding off about current events. Virtually every discussion connects indirectly to something Amazon sells, but the discussions themselves are interest driven, not product driven. The blogs are closely moderated, which means that abusive communication is deleted and posts about such issues as refunds and order tracking are silently redirected to the appropriate people at Amazon.

Through Omnivoracious, Amazon gives its customers a forum that delivers significant added value. Participating in the forum gives the company's customers additional information and opinions about topics that are important to them, and it delivers an important social experience that promotes a sense of identity and belonging. The forum also gives the one of the world's largest retailers a constant stream of new information about what's most important to its customers!

Could you give your customers a forum where they can gather with others who use what you sell and discuss issues that they feel are important?

! **ART #93**: Create and support forums both online and "in real life" that deliver added value and a sense of belonging.

! **ART #94**: Consider innovative sponsorship partnerships that deliver more value-added benefits for your customers, such as Amazon's partnership with publishers for certain online reading groups.

LET CUSTOMERS EXPRESS THEMSELVES IN USER GROUPS

Amazement Revolutionary: Apple, Inc.
Enterprise Focus: Computers and software, digital electronics, digital distribution
Headquarters Location: Cupertino, CA
Website: www.apple.com
What You Need to Know: An innovative leader in computers, consumer electronics, software, and customer service, Apple Inc., which was founded in 1976, employs 34,000 people and was named one of the nation's best places to work by Glassdoor in 2010.

Before we begin, let me acknowledge that Apple is one of those companies that consistently implements all seven of the Amazement Strategies in this book. It could easily have served as a role model in any of those seven areas. I chose to focus on Apple's relationship to its user community because evangelism for Apple has become such an obvious, and sometimes inescapable, part of contemporary American life. If you use a personal computer and you aren't a member of the Apple community, I can predict with confidence that you know someone who is.

In our last role model example, we saw how Amazon sponsors and monitors a network of *topic*-driven online forums under the Omnivoracious domain. Now it's time to look at a much more *product*-focused, open-ended, freewheeling model: Apple's sprawling network of user groups.

Visit the Website for Apple usergroups, and you will be greeted with this message: "People who use Apple technologies have joined together in user groups all around the world. Hundreds of groups offer members the chance to become friends with other Apple product users, get questions answered, and have a lot of fun….Want technology to do more for you? Join the club. Find a user group near you."[3]

User groups started out as face-to-face gatherings, and many of them still are. The groups provide essential service and product guidance to hundreds of thousands of Apple customers and are clearly an important part of the Apple business plan—but they are not run by the company! Independent volunteers manage the user-group sites, which have names like "Macintosh Guild" and "Boston Final Cut Pro User Group." Apple's ties to its community of loyal users are strong enough for it to off-load much of its product-focused customer service traffic to communities (both virtual and face-to-face) that are administered by "senior" Apple customers, not paid staff!

This mutually beneficial arrangement means leaving behind the editorial control that characterizes the Omnivoracious discussion groups mentioned previously. Apple fanatics have very strong opinions about the company's products, and not all of those opinions take the form of love letters to Apple. Some of the posts composed by members of the user community are hostile toward the company. A few of these negative reviews are downright caustic.

A similar trend is evident at the App Store, Apple's popular online source for free and low-cost software designed exclusively for the iPad and iPhone. Users of the App Store (which Apple owns and operates) are encouraged to use the site to give frank evaluations of how the software and the technology itself performs. Reviewers don't hold back. When they spot a problem with the software, the technology, or any combination, they write about the problem and don't mince words.

Apple leaves the negative reviews up for at least two reasons. First, if there really is a problem, they want it identified and, if possible, fixed as soon as possible. Leaving negative reviews up facilitates that process. Second, Apple views constructive conflict as an important part of its culture, both internally (among Apple employees) and externally (within the fanatically loyal, and often emotional, community of Apple users).

By giving people license to vent and resisting the temptation to remove or edit posts simply because they're critical of the company, Apple has managed to create a remarkable sense of belonging and advocacy in both its workforce and its user base. Conflict, after all, is a big part of the evangelism that takes place on behalf of the Apple brand: people don't just like Apple computers, they actively *dislike* and evangelize *against* the Windows operating system.

The culture of advocacy at Apple is rooted, not just in great products, but also in constructive engagement about those products. That means listening when users point out problems and flaws, suggest creative solutions, and champion new ideas.

Could a user group help you to build your community?

!   ART #95: Look for opportunities to partner with, communicate with, and promote independent user groups of your product or service.

!   **ART #96:** Monitor negative reviews in user groups and through social media channels like Twitter for potential service problems that you can rectify.

!   **ART #97:** Don't try to remove negative comments about your company from discussion groups, social media channels, and other points of contact with your community. Hearing about the good, the bad, and the ugly will help you do a better job of serving your very best customers.

CHARITY CAN STRENGTHEN YOUR BRAND

Amazement Revolutionary: Virgin Unite
Enterprise Focus: Charitable/nonprofit
Headquarters Location: London, England
Website: www.virginunite.com
What You Need to Know: Sir Richard Branson's charitable foundation, Virgin Unite is an umbrella organization that funds and promotes multiple charities; its stated goal is to "unite people to tackle tough social and environmental problems in an entrepreneurial way." It was founded in 2004, although many of the charities it promotes were founded before that date. It employs approximately twenty full-time employees.

What comes to mind when you hear the name "Richard Branson"? I first think of an amazing and successful businessman who loves adventure. I also think of David versus Goliath, with David not only beating Goliath, but having fun doing so.

Richard Branson, who is (according to *Fortune* magazine) the 212th richest person in the world somehow still manages to get a global community of admirers to root for him as the underdog in a never-ending series of long-shot battles. If you're not yet familiar with him, what you need to know is that Sir Richard (the queen knighted him in 1999) is a restless, barrier-busting industrialist and adventurer of the kind that hasn't been seen since the glory days of Howard Hughes. After his own personal exploits, such as attempting to circle the globe in a balloon, he is perhaps best known for founding Virgin Atlantic Airways and the Virgin Megastores group of retail stores. However, the empire is much bigger than that. The parent company he presides over, the Virgin Group, licenses and/or operates over 360 companies that use the Virgin brand.

That brand always positions the Virgin product or service, which may be anything from a comic book to a credit card, as young, hip, irreverent, energetic, and intensely customer focused; the competition, by contrast, is positioned as old, complacent, huge, unfair, and generally clueless about what customers really want. For nearly four decades, Branson's favorite PR storyline has been that of the Little Guy versus Big Competition. He has used that timeless, effective attention-getting format since he launched his first business, a mail-order operation, as a teenager.

Knighted or not, billionaire or not, Branson remains his own best expression of the underdog Virgin brand: untraditional, cheeky, fun loving, and forever striving to beat the odds and slay Goliath. At any given moment, Goliath's identity is likely to change. Slaying him may mean setting the world speed record for crossing the English Channel, or it may mean winning market share from far more experienced competitors. (Branson knew next to nothing about the airline industry, for instance, when he launched Virgin Atlantic.)

It's not surprising, then, that Branson's charitable foundation supports both his brand and the vast global community of fans who have been rooting him on against various Big Unfair Competitors since at least the mid-1970s. The charitable arm of his empire is known as Virgin Unite, and it is a masterful blend of philanthropy, public relations, and brand promotion. Branson's double stroke of genius was expanding his community of consumer evangelists by building cause awareness and using the same successful promotional strategy he has used for the last several decades to build Virgin's *brand* awareness.

In the usual *for-profit* message, the Virgin product or service (say, Virgin Atlantic) challenges a Big Competitor (say, British Airways) on behalf of the consumer, and then makes the case that Virgin offers more value and more fun than the competitor does. In the *not-for-profit* version if the story, Virgin United tackles a Big Problem on behalf of humanity at large (say, improving the quality of health care in underdeveloped countries), and then makes the case that supporting the Virgin charity brings about more solutions and can be more fun than simply doing nothing.

The for-profit and not-for-profit messages are completely complementary. Virgin Unite both supports and expands the Virgin community of evangelists, because *all* Virgin consumers across all 360-plus Virgin businesses are also potential donors, advocates, and volunteers on behalf of a Virgin charity! And just as there are many Virgin-branded companies, there are many Virgin United charities to choose from.

In both the for-profit and non-profit realms, members of Branson's community are captivated enough by the David versus Goliath message to take notice, take action, and take on the job of evangelizing for Virgin.

Do your charitable efforts strengthen the loyalty your customers have to your brand?

! **ART #98**: Your involvement in charities (local and/or global) can enhance your customers' perceptions of your organization.

! **ART #99**: Promote your organization's charitable causes using the same themes you use to promote your brand in the for-profit realm.

! **ART #100**: You can create an even stronger relationship with your best customers by inspiring them to partner with you in your charitable efforts.

RECAP: AMAZEMENT STRATEGY #6—BUILD COMMUNITY

To implement this Amazement Strategy, try the following ideas:

- Enlist your most engaged customers to supply you with good ideas, as Harley-Davidson does.
- Use your brand to make an ethical statement about something that is genuinely important to you, your organization, and at least a portion of your customers, as Lush does.
- Build your brand promise around a single cause that defines your target market, as Pedro's Planet does.
- Simplify your product or service line to focus only on what your community of evangelists wants and has always loved, as In-N-Out Burger does.
- Give your customers a value-added discussion forum where they can gather to share views with and socialize with others who use what you sell, as Amazon does.
- Harness the power of independent user groups, as Apple does.
- Create an even stronger relationship with your best customers by inspiring them to partner with you in your charitable efforts, as Virgin Unite does.
- Key point: Listen to your best customers, support them, and respect them!

CHAPTER TEN

STRATEGY #7:
WALK THE WALK

Organizations that operate within the cult of amazement are guided by the same values up and down the organization. These values may emphasize different issues, depending on the company, but they always support the principle of *doing right by the customer*. Everyone in an amazing company strives to live by those values, from senior executives to the receptionist who answers the phone and from the founder of the enterprise to the employee who was just hired yesterday.

Walking the walk means acting in support of your organization's best values, all the time, no matter what, wherever you are in the pecking order.

In the American Express example, we saw how Jim Bush, the company's executive vice president of world service, is evaluated against the same standard that everyone else who reports to him is evaluated against: how likely are customers to recommend American Express to their own friends and family?

You might wonder how seriously someone at Bush's level actually takes such a standard. Allow me to share a true story that will help to clarify the issue.

When I began my first interview for this book with Jim Bush, I happened to mention that I was an American Express cardmember and that I had been one since 1984. Bush's first response was to ask me how my own personal experience as a cardmember has been and to find out if there was any issue he could help to address! I can still remember his words when I said that my experience with American Express had been superb. He said, "Remember, we're here to help!"

I was talking, not to an individual service rep, but to the executive vice president of world service of the American Express Company!

Before we even got started with our interview, Bush wanted to make sure the member he was talking to was feeling great about his company. If there was an issue that could possibly have *kept* me from feeling great, he wanted to *personally* ensure that it got fixed. Bush understood, on a personal level, a critical principle of the Amazement Revolution: *The values senior leadership models always cascade throughout the organization.* For American Express as a whole to be concerned about whether a customer has a good impression of the company, *Jim Bush* has to be concerned about whether a customer has a good impression of the company.

When the values support doing right by the customer, and when the entire organization is aligned on those values and consistently takes action on them, I call that walking the walk. Walking the walk means your organization doesn't just talk a good game. It consistently *acts* on the right values, up and down the company.

Here are some more of my favorite examples of companies that walk the walk.

KNOW YOUR VALUES

Amazement Revolutionary: Zappos.com, Inc.
Enterprise Focus: Retail

Headquarters Location: Henderson, NV

Website: www.zappos.com

What You Need to Know: A subsidiary of Amazon, Zappos recently grossed over $1 billion in annual sales. It is the largest online shoe store; it also sells handbags, apparel, eyewear, and accessories. It was founded in 1999 and employs over 1,600 people. Zappos was named to *Fortune* magazine's list of 100 Best Companies to Work For in 2009.

I have two favorite quotes from Tony Hsieh, the visionary Zappos founder and CEO. The first is about customer service, which is of course what this book is about; the quote may give you some insight into why Zappos has been as successful as it has. Tony said, "We interview people for a cultural fit. We want people who are passionate about what Zappos is about—service. I don't care if they're passionate about shoes."[1] This quote helps us to focus on Hsieh's concept of *core committable values*. By "core committable," he means that the value in question, in this case passion for service, is a value that you must be fully *committed* to in order to work at Zappos. If Zappos hires you, it's because you really are consistently committed to that value. If for some reason you *stop* being consistently committed to service, Zappos will fire you. Simple as that.

My other favorite quote from Tony Hsieh connects to transparency, another of Zappos's core committable values: "The best way to have an open-door policy is not to have a door in the first place."[2] Yes, that means what you think it means. If you ever visit the Las Vegas headquarters of the breakthrough online shoe and apparel retailer, you will find that Hsieh's workspace literally has no doors. He's not hiding in a big corner office. He's in a cubicle, out on the floor with the rest of the team, working collaboratively.

Questioned about this arrangement by PBS's Tavis Smiley, Hsieh confirmed Zappos's floor plan and said, "It's not just me; almost all employees have a cubicle....Definitely you can overhear each other's phone calls, and so it just helps make you feel like you're really part of the action.

For me, I think if I were in a corner office or in an office anywhere I'd be pretty lonely."[3]

This open door, access-to-all-executives philosophy is part of the larger value of transparency. Transparency is simply how Zappos operates, whether you're talking about Tony Hsieh or anyone else. If you're not willing to model transparency in everything you do, then you've picked the wrong company to work for. End of story!

Zappos is deeply invested in these two values—passion for service and transparency—but they aren't the *only* two values that they expect employees to model for each other, for customers, and for the outside world. Here are some others:

- Embrace and drive change.
- Create fun and a little weirdness.
- Be adventurous, creative, and open-minded.
- Pursue growth and learning.
- Build open and honest relationships with communication.
- Build a positive team and family spirit.
- Do more with less.
- Be passionate and determined.
- Be humble.[4]

These core values affect the experience the customer receives from Zappos, and they also help to define the type of personality Zappos tries to hire.

Do these have to be *your* organization's core values? Of course not. But to operate within the cult of amazement, your organization must have *some* core values that everyone understands, discusses, and sees modeled regularly by senior management and everyone else in your organization.

If your organization *says* that transparency and open communication are among the most important values for anyone who works for you, but no one ever sees your senior executives because they're all hidden away in corner offices, then there's a problem. Either the core values you've identified need to change, or the working patterns of your senior executives have to change!

> *Does your organization have a set of core values that helps*
> *you to deliver the right experience to customers and also*
> *helps you identify the kind of personality you want to hire?*
> *Does everyone in the organization act in accordance*
> *with those values, without exception?*

! **ART #101**: Identify core committable values—values that you will hire for or fire for—that support your organization's service mission.

! **ART #102**: Make passion for service a core committable value.

! **ART #103**: Transparency and open communication are important core committable values that can support customer-focused organizations when modeled from the top down.

SET THE EXAMPLE

Amazement Revolutionary: The Walt Disney Company
Enterprise Focus: Media and park/resort conglomerate
Headquarters Location: Burbank, CA
Website: www.disney.com
What You Need to Know: Measured by revenue, the Walt Disney Company is the world's largest media and entertainment conglomerate. The company is named after its legendary founder, who was a pioneer in animation, motion pictures, television, theme parks, and customer service. The firm employs over 150,000 people.

Once you get to be CEO of a Fortune 100 company, you shouldn't have to worry about things like personally picking up the trash anymore, right?

Wrong.

At least, that's the answer you'll hear if you ask Michael Eisner, former CEO of the Disney Company. In his book *Work in Progress*, Eisner recalls that, whenever he came across a piece of trash on the ground at one of the Disney theme parks (or anywhere else, for that matter), he always tried to send the right signal to the Disney employees, who are also known as cast members. How did he send that message? Instead of simply ignoring the garbage or instructing someone else to pick it up, Eisner got into the habit of picking the trash up himself.[5]

He called setting this kind of example "stooping to excellence." The idea was, and is, breathtakingly simple. Since senior executives inevitably model behaviors that get passed through to the rest of the organization, those managers should set the example of personally attending to the "little things" that can make a big difference. In other words, if we want the rest of the team to deliver excellence in any area, such as keeping the workplace, a public area, or the theme park spotlessly clean, we must set a *visible* personal example in that area—and we must be ready to do that, not just once, but on a regular basis.

"Little things" like seeing the CEO bend over and pick up a candy wrapper are actually very big things when it comes to building and sustaining organizational culture! Even if you are not the CEO of a major corporation, you can and should look for opportunities to *act* like a true leader by stooping to excellence. Once you set the personal example that proves through action what you really stand for, you can expect other employees, especially those on the front line, to buy into those same values. On the other hand, if you prove by your actions that you *don't* buy into those values, then you shouldn't be surprised if your people dismiss all your talk as *just* talk.

By picking up the trash himself, Eisner set the right *visible* example, just as Tony Hsieh did with his equally visible personal example in support of the value of transparency.

The real power of Eisner's embrace of this idea lies in the fact that it wasn't really his idea at all. *Walt Disney himself* is the originator of the stooping to excellence concept and of an even larger organizational principle that motivated Eisner. That principle requires Disney management to forget about whose "job" it is to pick up a stray piece of trash, welcome a guest, resolve a traffic problem, or address any other problem. This principle is an extension of the Disney service legacy, a fact that Eisner himself is quick to point out. Disney called this team-driven success principle "all for one and one for all."

Managers, Walt Disney argued, are part of the team, too. That means they should be just as ready, willing, and able to step into customer service situations, keep the park clean, and connect directly with guests as anyone else. In fact, a critical part of the training for Disney's senior managers is to get out to a theme park, put on one of those huge Disney character costumes, and stroll through the theme park, entertaining the guests along the way. Now that's walking the walk!

What do your team members see you doing in support of your stated customer service values?

! **ART #104**: Make sure management and senior executives have direct, regular, face-to-face exposure to the customer service environment, and that they consistently model the same behaviors and meet the same standards they expect from front-line employees.

! **ART #105**: Senior management must not expect employees to do anything they themselves haven't done and are ready to do again if necessary. For example, if the CEO is not willing to take a call from a customer on the toll-free line, there's a problem.

! **ART #106**: "All for one and one for all" customer service is everyone's job. Service is not a department. It's a philosophy!

PUT YOUR MONEY WHERE YOUR MOUTH IS

Amazement Revolutionary: Stew Leonard's
Enterprise Focus: Grocery/retail
Headquarters Location: Norwalk, CT
Website: www.stewleonards.com
What You Need to Know: The innovative dairy and grocery chain, which was founded in 1969 and employs approximately 1,800 people has a no-layoff policy. It has consistently been named one of *Fortune* magazine's 100 Best Companies to Work For.

Top executives at this Norwalk, Connecticut-based specialty grocery chain needed to hold the line on costs in order to maintain its policy of not downsizing the workforce. How did they get the funds? By putting a freeze on their own salaries! The cash freed up as a result of this pay freeze not only ensured that the company wouldn't have to lay anyone off—it also paid for a round of pay raises during one of the most intense economic downturns in recent memory! Hourly employees got a 4% hike; salaried workers outside of top management got a 3% boost.

Am I saying you need to freeze or cut executive salaries? Of course not! But I am saying that you have to find some dramatic way to prove that you are willing to go the extra mile for your employees and are totally committed to them. Senior management at Stew Leonard definitely did that!

What bold gesture can you make to your employees that will prove your commitment to them?

! ART #107: If you expect your employees to go the extra mile for your customers, you must prove that you are willing to go the extra mile for them!

DELIVER TOUGH NEWS IN PERSON

Amazement Revolutionary: NetApp

Enterprise Focus: Computer storage and data management

Headquarters Location: Sunnyvale, CA

Website: www.netapp.com

What You Need to Know: Founded in 1992, in recent years, the company has consistently ranked in the top fifty of *Fortune* magazine's annual list of 100 Best Companies to Work For. It employs over 8,000 people.

NetApp, an innovative California-based computer storage and data management firm, faced some serious marketplace challenges. The company's leaders decided their competitive position demanded a serious strategic reassessment. The new plan they came up with necessitated a 5% cut in the company's workforce.

Instead of doing what some companies do in that situation, which is send out an impersonal message or leave the job of delivering the news to mid-level managers, NetApp took a very different approach. Members of the company's senior management team hit the road and made personal visits to twenty-six regional offices in thirteen countries so they could personally explain what was happening, why it was happening, and what the company was doing to make the transition as painless as possible for those being let go.

The result: a workforce that didn't lose weeks or months of productivity to the paranoia and rumor trading that typically accompanies a downsizing campaign. By putting the facts on the table, delivering difficult news and taking questions in person, and offering a severance package that employees perceived as fair, the top executives at NetApp kept the cult of amazement alive.

NetApp proved that even a company going through a period of redefinition can keep its internal lines of communication open, keep people motivated and focused on the future, and most importantly, keep on delivering on commitments to both employees and customers.

> *How does your organization handle the difficult task of delivering bad news?*

! **ART #108**: If you are a leader, you must deliver tough news in person. Don't leave the job to others.

! **ART #109**: An informed workforce is more confident and effective than an uninformed workforce, even when the news it has to process is difficult.

! **ART #110**: When you have difficult news to deliver, do it fast. Don't let rumors or paranoia set in.

LIVE YOUR MISSION

Amazement Revolutionary: Costco Wholesale Corporation
Enterprise Focus: Membership warehouse club retail chain
Headquarters Location: Issaquah, WA
Website: www.costco.com
What You Need to Know: Founded in 1983, Costco currently has more than 147,000 employees and operates in 563 locations throughout North America, Asia, and Australia.

Retail giant Costco is the ninth-largest store chain on the planet and the largest membership-driven warehouse store chain in the United States. The company recently cleared over $1 billion in net annual income. You might think that its CEO would run the company from an office setting that speaks the language of luxury.

You'd be wrong. James Sinegal, cofounder and CEO of Costco, speaks the language of thrift. He would be more accurately called Costco's penny pincher in chief, a significant role because he leads a company whose success is built on pinching pennies. That $1.75 billion in net income Costco reported resulted from *$74 billion* in annual sales. Do the math and you will realize that Costco works on very thin margins. Sinegal likes it that way! Thriftiness is part of his personality and part of his vision for the company, and he makes sure that every signal he sends to employees and other stakeholders is consistent with that penny-pinching vision.

Sinegal has no band of followers who trail his every move—a rarity among CEOs of companies on the S&P 500. He visits Costco facilities in person, so he can ask store managers directly about how they are running the store and how they are moving the most popular merchandise. His own workplace is definitely short on frills. His office overlooks the parking lot of his company's headquarters in Issaquah, Washington. When visitors step into his office and Sinegal invites them to sit down, they are often astonished to learn that he means they should take a seat on standard-issue folding chairs.

Sinegal's unassuming office setting, his communication style, and even his comparatively modest compensation package would be completely out of place if he were CEO of most other multibillion dollar corporations. As it happens, though, all those elements are all in complete alignment with Costco's personality—which happens to be Sinegal's personality, too: committed, unimpressed by frills and extras, and perpetually eager to save a buck or two. Sinegal's personality is impossible to distinguish from his company's personality, and that's a conscious choice. Both he and his company are committed to a clear mission: *deliver high value on low margins, no matter what.* This approach has allowed Costco to establish an important competitive advantage in the brutally competitive retail market.

A rarity among major American retailers, Costco limits its markup on all items sold to a maximum level—15%, although most items are sold at markups far below that number. If the company can make those margins work, then Sinegal makes them work. That means Costco members count on high value, return to the warehouse store, and evangelize on behalf of the company.

Numbers are nice, and Costco's are stellar. For instance, it was the first company in history to grow from zero to $3 billion in sales in less than six years. But numbers only go so far, and they are incapable of building or sustaining a culture of amazement. Sinegal has built a company with a personality that *is* powerful enough to sustain amazement. Costco's lean, value-focused, service-driven, no-frills culture is not public relations or double-talk. It really is how Jim Sinegal personally operates. Which explains why it really is how *Costco* operates, both for employees and for customers!

Does your organization's leader have a personality that supports the mission?

! **ART #111**: If you are a leader, it is imperative that your personality complement your organization's mission and set the tone for all the organization's interactions with customers.

! **ART #112**: Walking the walk means you live and breathe your company's mission, vision, and values, and that your personality is congruent with what your company stands for.

SHARE YOUR STORY

Amazement Revolutionary: L.L.Bean, Inc.
Enterprise Focus: Retail
Headquarters Location: Freeport, ME
Website: www.llbean.com
What You Need to Know: In addition to its many other accolades, the clothing and outdoor equipment retailer was recently ranked the number-one provider of customer service by the National Retail Federation Foundation/American Express Customer Service Survey.

This was the third consecutive year L.L.Bean led the survey. The company was also named the number-one Bloomberg Businessweek Customer Service Champ. L.L.Bean was founded in 1912.

Every employee at the Maine-based outdoor equipment and apparel retailer L.L.Bean knows the remarkable true story of how the company was founded in the early part of the last century. In fact, learning and sharing that legendary story is an important part of *becoming* an employee at L.L.Bean, which is today a leader in customer service and one of the most respected and trusted retailers in the country.

Back in 1911, Leon Leonwood (L.L.) Bean, an avid hunter, came home with cold, wet feet and decided to do something about it besides warm himself in front of the fireplace. He got a local cobbler to sew leather uppers onto a pair of rubber boots, inventing a waterproof boot he called the Maine hunting shoe. The footwear, he concluded, was perfect for exploring the forests and streams of rural Maine. L.L. decided to build a company around the product.

To launch his business, he created a memorable direct-mail piece that read, "You cannot expect success hunting deer or moose if your feet are not properly dressed. The Maine Hunting Shoe is designed by a hunter who has tramped the Maine woods for the last 18 years. We guarantee them to give perfect satisfaction in every way."[6]

A hundred orders came in for the Maine Hunting Shoe; however, because of a manufacturing defect, *ninety* of those customers eventually demanded refunds on the product! True to his word, L.L. refunded the money. He then fixed the manufacturing problem, sent out more brochures, and began building a rock-solid reputation as a trustworthy source of both outdoor equipment and sound advice for hikers and hunters.

Although this story sounds like an example of a customer service disaster, it has actually been the source of everything amazing the company has achieved in the century that followed. Why? Because the story demonstrates the company's core value to everyone who hears it. That core value, by the way, is also the L.L.Bean brand promise to consumers: Guaranteed. You have our word. The whole company is built around and aligned on that promise!

As a direct result of his employees hearing, understanding, internalizing, and sharing that impossible-to-forget company legend, L.L.Bean created a special kind of culture, one that is completely aligned on the core value of *following through on commitments.* The founder may be gone, but thanks to that story, the organization as a whole still walks the walk and follows his personal example.

As Leon Gorman, the company's president from 1967 to 2001, put it: "Word-of-mouth advertising and customer satisfaction were critical to L.L.'s way of thinking. To hear that one of his products failed was a genuine shock to his system. That customer was a real person to L.L. and he'd put his trust in the L.L.Bean catalog."

Do you have a story that embodies the values that employees must live up to at your organization?

! **ART #113**: Find your story. It should be one that supports your values and your organization's promise to customers. Share the story constantly; make knowing it and retelling it part of what it means to be a part of your organization.

FOLLOW THE EMPLOYEE GOLDEN RULE

Amazement Revolutionary: Southwest Airlines Co.

Enterprise Focus: Commercial passenger airline

Headquarters Location: Dallas, TX

Website: www.southwest.com

What You Need to Know: The airline, founded in 1971, is frequently ranked as one of America's most admired companies. It has won awards for customer service delivered within the travel sector, for employee satisfaction, and for corporate citizenship. Southwest employs over 35,000 people.

When iconic Southwest Airlines co-founder Herb Kelleher stepped down as chairman of the board, he left a legacy that was focused on creating amazing customer service. Kelleher built and sustained a successful company at every level, a company that has maintained a simple priority over the years: employees come first. He himself lived up to that principle during the years he led the company.

This employees-first approach was an extremely controversial first principle, as management philosophies go. But Kelleher really meant it, and he insisted on it for sound strategic reasons. **When you build a company around the idea of taking care of employees, then taking care of customers becomes easier for everyone.** As Kelleher himself put it:

"Years ago, business gurus used to apply the business school conundrum to me: 'Who comes first? Your shareholders, your employees, or your customers?' I said, 'Well, that's easy,' but my response was heresy at that time. I said employees come first and if employees are treated right, they treat the outside world right, the outside world uses the company's product again, and that makes the shareholders happy. That really is the way that it works, and it's not a conundrum at all."[7]

Truer words were never spoken. This outlook on service—that it starts with service to employees—became embedded within the working culture of Southwest Airlines. Kelleher's insistence on this point is, I believe, the real reason that airline has succeeded so memorably at a time when so many of its competitors have faltered. Following this philosophy, Kelleher built a community of employees who walked the walk, and he eventually handed the company over to executives who walked the walk. The transition was seamless—one of the reasons why Southwest is still an amazing organization!

The legacy Kelleher left behind at Southwest really is nothing more or less than the Employee Golden Rule that I mentioned earlier and that I've been advocating for years: **treat your employees the way you'd want**

them to treat customers—maybe even better. This rule is worth repeating and memorizing!

A recent poll of employee satisfaction at Southwest, conducted three years after Kelleher's departure, gives the organization a rating of 4.5 out of 5.0—an incredibly high satisfaction rate for the airline industry. At the end of the day, that's the legacy I think all of us should be trying to pass along to our service organizations: that our employees love showing up for work every day! If we follow the Employee Golden Rule, we can make that kind of workplace a reality. And that, believe it or not, is the ultimate revolution in customer service.

> *What would happen if you consistently treated your employees the way you wanted them to treat customers—maybe even better?*

! **ART #114**: Everyone must walk the walk when it comes to modeling customer service, either to external customers or internal customers (employees). This principle is extremely important because if you are not on the front line yourself, you are in a role that supports the front line, directly or indirectly!

! **ART #115**: Make sure everyone, at all levels, practices the Employee Golden Rule: treat your fellow employees the way you want the customer treated—maybe even better.

RECAP: AMAZEMENT STRATEGY #7—WALK THE WALK

To implement this Amazement Strategy, try these ideas:

- Identify core commitment values, as Zappos does.
- "Stoop to excellence" and model the behavior for your employees, as the Walt Disney Company does.

- Prove to your employees that you are willing to go the extra mile for them, as Stew Leonard's does.
- Deliver tough news in person, as NetApp does.
- Hire top people whose personalities complement the organization's mission and set the tone for its interactions with customers, as Costco has. Ideally, all employees would present a personality that supports and complements the company mission, but top executives are a good group to start with.
- Share a company story that supports both your values and your organization's promise to customers, as L.L.Bean does.
- Treat your fellow employees the way you want the customer treated, maybe even better, as Southwest Airlines does.
- Key point: Walking the walk means acting in support of your organization's best values all the time, no matter what.

AFTERWORD

Between these covers, we've gone from a child's birthday party magic-show business to some of the most successful enterprises on Earth, many of them multibillion-dollar operations. And you know what? The same thread runs through each and every example I have shared with you in this book.

Whether I was telling you about the first time I sent a thank-you note after doing a magic show for a paying customer or the tough little Internet hosting company that prevented a disaster by assuming that a customer's problem was *their* problem or the way a charismatic CEO of one of the world's great airlines created a culture that was focused on delivering amazing customer service *or any of the other true stories in this book*, I was really telling you *one* true story.

We can condense that story into one simple sentence:

Treat your customers the way they should and want to be treated, and they will come back again and again.

That's what the Amazement Revolution is in a nutshell, and it's also what my parents were teaching me when they emphasized how important it was to do the right thing by my very first customer. Isn't it amazing that an outfit as simple as a child's magic-show business could harness the most important lesson of all in the realm of customer service?

Because I was willing to launch and support an Amazement Revolution at the age of twelve, I was able to build a real business, in the form of my speaking and training company.

Because companies like American Express, Nordstrom, Zappos, and all the other role models you've read about and learned from in this book were willing to launch and support their own Amazement Revolutions, they confirmed their status as premier customer service organizations.

Now it's time for you to decide: Are you willing to launch and support an Amazement Revolution?

I sincerely hope the answer is yes.

You have been given a lot of ideas to consider. In closing, I want to leave you with *one* last reminder. This one idea has the power to transform your entire organization. **At the end of the day, creating amazement is really very simple. Be *consistently* better than average!**

Always be amazing!

Shep Hyken

Shep Hyken, CSP, CPAE
Chief Amazement Officer
Shepard Presentations LLC

P.S. I hope you will share your own Amazement Revolution stories with me! Please visit my Website and stay in touch at www.amazementrevolution.com.

PART FOUR

CREATE YOUR OWN
AMAZEMENT REVOLUTION

APPENDIX A:

THE ART OF AMAZEMENT
TO-DO LIST

T his is a summary of the specific best practices that you have read about in this book. Use them to create your own unique to-do lists and as a precursor to the **Amazement Brainstorm Worksheets** you will find in appendix B.

AMAZEMENT REVOLUTION TAKEAWAYS FROM AMERICAN EXPRESS

☐ **ART #1:** Start thinking of your customers as members of a special group; consider a change in the labels you use to describe them, both internally and externally.

☐ **ART #2:** Brainstorm ways to deliver amenities that will take the customer experience to another level.

☐ **ART #3:** Invest in creating the membership experience.

☐ **ART #4:** Give your people a greater sense of personal fulfillment by giving them the training and the autonomy they need to solve problems and make good recommendations. Don't try to micromanage their every word and deed.

☐ **ART #5:** Respect and embrace the uniqueness of each of your employees.

☐ **ART #6**: Issue a professional challenge that inspires team players and makes them look forward to what's next.

☐ **ART #7**: Ask your team what should change.

☐ **ART #8**: Don't subsidize poor performance.

☐ **ART #9**: Throw away the script; give your people more autonomy to identify and solve problems.

☐ **ART #10**: Change internal job title terminology.

☐ **ART #11**: Empathetically solve existing problems. Then proactively look for unanticipated problems to solve.

☐ **ART #12**: Use crises and Moments of Misery as opportunities to build or expand the partnership.

☐ **ART #13**: Strive for partner relationships with customers, with your employees, and with your vendors.

☐ **ART #14**: Wherever possible, identify and emphasize core values you share with your partners.

☐ **ART #15**: Look outside your industry for good talent.

☐ **ART #16**: Don't be afraid to reassign (or part company with) people who don't belong in customer-facing positions.

☐ **ART #17**: Periodically reevaluate your compensation system. Consider making customer feedback one of the major drivers.

☐ **ART #18**: There is no such thing as a transaction. The word transaction implies a clear starting point and an equally clear ending point. In the cult of amazement, however, any transaction is simply a transition into the next potential Moment of Magic.

☐ **ART #19**: Don't pressure employees to close customer interactions before they have a chance to build a relationship with the customer.

☐ **ART #20**: There are probably hundreds, if not thousands, of ways to effectively follow through. Empower people to find some of them. Recognize and consider rewarding them when they do.

☐ **ART #21**: Create goals that inspire and engage your internal evangelists (employees).

☐ **ART #22**: Develop value-added privileges, rewards, and amenities to offer your customers as a way to build community.

☐ **ART #23**: Model congruence with the right customer-focused values at all times.

☐ **ART #24**: Start a congruence movement within your organization. Everyone should walk the walk!

☐ **ART #25**: Identify customer feedback that's both objective and measurable that everyone in your organization, regardless of rank, can use as a benchmark.

☐ **ART #26**: Consider tying compensation to Fred Reichheld's Ultimate Question: "On a scale of one to ten, what is the likelihood that you would recommend us to a friend or associate?"

AMAZEMENT REVOLUTION TAKEAWAYS: PROVIDE MEMBERSHIP

☐ **ART #27**: Build processes that make your customers feel special by giving them recognition, reassurance, and respect.

☐ **ART #28**: Find out what your customers value most and find hard to get. Build value-added "membership" offerings around that.

☐ **ART #29**: Consider a two-track service strategy that aims to turn casual customers into loyal members.

☐ **ART #30**: Identify first-time customers and create a special welcoming or initiation ritual for them.

☐ **ART #31**: Membership can allow your customers to send important messages about their values, traditions, and standards to the outside world. Build a "membership" experience that makes your customers want to say to themselves and others, "Look at the kind of company I keep."

☐ **ART #32**: Introduce customers to your organization by appealing to a powerful sense of belonging. This is not just good customer service, it's also good marketing!

☐ **ART #33**: Make access to hard-to-get resources, people, experience, ideas, and tools a benefit of doing business with you.

☐ **ART #34**: Make changes in your organizational terminology with words like "member" and "club" that will help keep both staff and customers focused on expectations of a high level of service.

AMAZEMENT REVOLUTION TAKEAWAYS: HAVE SERIOUS FUN

☐ **ART #35**: Once you engage your team with FUN by giving them work that is fulfilling, that utilizes their unique talents, and that is challenging, they will engage with your customer service mission.

☐ **ART #36**: Engage your employees the way you want them to engage your customers, and you will start to create employee loyalty.

☐ **ART #37**: Use regularly scheduled all-team meetings to energize and connect with everyone.

☐ **ART #38**: Give your most creative people the opportunity to spend at least part of their time on projects they choose that will also create value for the customer. This approach focuses on the employee's uniqueness. As a result, you will have more engaged and fulfilled employees—and that's good for business!

☐ **ART #39**: Build and support a culture that supports flexibility in the workplace. This flexibility could express itself in terms of scheduling, working from home, or even the décor in an employee's workspace. Leverage this culture to attract and retain the best talent.

☐ **ART #40**: Create a program for employees to recognize, acknowledge, and reward their peers for superior service. Encourage employees to display the cards they receive in their work area. This kind of public praise creates a sense of fulfillment!

☐ **ART #41**: Once you've hired people you can trust, let them know you trust them. Don't just say it. Prove it, and people will reward you with their loyalty.

☐ **ART #42**: If you want intense loyalty from your customers, you must be intensely loyal to your employees.

☐ **ART #43**: Have fun; find lots of reasons to celebrate. Yes, small successes and employee milestones are worth celebrating! A culture of celebration can lead to deep fulfillment, long-term employee retention, and an improved customer experience.

☐ **ART #44**: Even companies that sell the most serious products and services have reasons to celebrate.

☐ **ART #45**: Change the vocabulary, and you change the attitude and the atmosphere!

AMAZEMENT REVOLUTION TAKEAWAYS: CULTIVATE PARTNERSHIP

☐ **ART #46**: When you spot a customer who's in crisis (or about to be), take the initiative to resolve the crisis or alert the customer to the crisis before the customer comes to you.

☐ **ART #47**: Make it your organization's goal to amaze every customer, on every engagement, with complete integrity—no exceptions. Once you begin working toward this goal, you will create opportunities to win much deeper business relationships and support new partnerships. Remember: It's all about taking care of the customer!

☐ **ART #48**: Make the customer's problem your problem.

☐ **ART #49**: Look beyond business for a way to connect with your customer at a deeper, personal level. Doing this can help you create both evangelism and intense, unshakeable loyalty.

☐ **ART #50**: Create confidence. Deliver service that's consistent and so good that customers make you their partner because they can count on you, without fail, every time.

☐ **ART #51**: Identify and recognize repeat customers. Make them feel special and amaze them.

☐ **ART #52**: Identify what customers like least about your industry. (The problems you uncover might not necessarily be about you and your company.) Work to eliminate any and all of these customer preconceptions.

☐ **ART #53**: If doing so can fit into your business model, go to the customer (instead of making him or her come to you).

☐ **ART #54**: Give a little more than the customer thinks you are going to give. Little extras you don't charge for can go a long way!

☐ **ART #55**: Amazing levels of service can help make price less relevant.

☐ **ART #56:** Sometimes, all you have to do is what people would expect you to do. The ability to consistently meet a certain minimum expected standard can give you and your organization a massive competitive advantage.

☐ **ART #57:** Be on time, every time. No exceptions.

☐ **ART #58:** Knowledge can create credibility and confidence, which are essential ingredients in any partnership relationship.

☐ **ART #59:** Being a trusted advisor doesn't always mean having all the answers. It means knowing where to get the answers and knowing how to use the information you uncover on someone else's behalf.

☐ **ART #60:** Create a brand promise that is so strong and so compelling that it makes your customers want to become your partner.

☐ **ART #61:** Align your team on the brand promise so they understand it even better than your customers do. They must live it, breathe it, and deliver it.

AMAZEMENT REVOLUTION TAKEAWAYS: HIRE RIGHT

☐ **ART #62:** Hire for attitude first, skills second.

☐ **ART #63:** Don't be afraid to use an unconventional hiring process, such as an audition, to identify the best personality fit for the job.

☐ **ART #64:** Use the interview process to figure out whether the applicant will best fit into your culture.

☐ **ART #65:** In the recruiting, hiring, and retention process, look for the "true believers" of your product, philosophy, mission, and values. Whether or not they have formal sales experience, these people can become your best sales force.

☐ **ART #66:** At the very best companies to work for, employees don't just "show up for work"—they evangelize on behalf of the organization.

☐ **ART #67:** Define what customer service means to you and your organization. During the job interview, ask candidates to give you their definition of customer service, so you can see how well their definition aligns with your organization's.

☐ **ART #68:** Keep it in the family! Create an internal employee referral program. The best job leads can come from your current employees.

☐ **ART #69**: If people don't want to recommend your company as a potential employer to their qualified friends and family members, you should find out why not!

☐ **ART #70**: Your best new employee just might be one of your customers—or a referral from one of your customers.

☐ **ART #71**: Ask job candidates to observe their potential future working environments. Get their feedback about what's working and what could be improved. You will learn a lot about the applicant and maybe even something about your organization.

☐ **ART #72**: Send new hires a positive and authentic personal message from senior management to welcome them to their new job.

☐ **ART #73**: Apply the after-experience principle to your recruitment and hiring campaign by giving new hires some type of gift. Keep it simple; you don't need to make the gift extravagant. Your gift should add to the welcoming experience and set the tone for how fellow employees, not just customers, are treated.

AMAZEMENT REVOLUTION TAKEAWAYS: CREATE A MEMORABLE AFTER-EXPERIENCE

☐ **ART #74**: Create an after-experience by following through in a way that is unexpected, appreciated, and memorable.

☐ **ART #75**: A carefully chosen gift or token of appreciation can show that you really care about an individual customer.

☐ **ART #76**: The perfect gift doesn't have to be expensive or extravagant. It just needs to be right for the occasion, for your business, and for your customer.

☐ **ART #77**: In today's fast-paced world, a personalized thank-you note is often unexpected, sometimes memorable, and always appreciated.

☐ **ART #78**: Recognize and celebrate the big days in your customers' lives, such as birthdays and anniversaries. By the way, this is easier to do than ever before, thanks to social media applications like Facebook that list such dates.

☐ **ART #79**: Reward your customers with small gifts of appreciation that will reinforce your brand and make people positively reflect on their experience with you.

☐ **ART #80**: A thoughtful, well-chosen, and unexpected contact during slow times or in the off-season can create a memorable after-experience.

☐ **ART #81**: Sometimes a creative promotion can also be a great after-experience. For this to happen, the promotion must be appreciated, must make the customer reflect on a recent positive experience, and must create a sense of anticipation.

☐ **ART #82**: After a customer's initial purchase experience, schedule a follow-up meeting, in person or over the phone, that delivers a value-added benefit that distinguishes you from the competition.

☐ **ART #83**: Use follow-up calls to accomplish two important goals: first, to let your customer know that he or she is appreciated; and second, to find out how you're doing.

☐ **ART #84**: When you're finished with your follow-up call, the customer should feel that the call was more about listening to and thanking him or her, and less about gathering information.

AMAZEMENT REVOLUTION TAKEAWAYS: BUILD COMMUNITY

☐ **ART #85**: Respect your customer base enough to listen to them and learn what's important to them.

☐ **ART #86**: When times are tough, remember that listening to your community of evangelists is more important than ever.

☐ **ART #87**: Bring your best customers into your research and development process.

☐ **ART #88**: Learn as much as you can, as often as you can, about the lifestyle choices your customers associate with your products and services.

☐ **ART #89**: Use your brand to make an ethical statement about something that is genuinely important to you, your organization, and a portion (if not all) of your customers.

☐ **ART #90:** Build or rebuild your business around a cause that inspires a community of passionate customers.

☐ **ART #91:** It is better to be great at one thing than to be average or mediocre at many.

☐ **ART #92:** Simplify. Focus relentlessly on giving your community of evangelists exactly what it loves.

☐ **ART #93:** Create and support forums both online and "in real life" that deliver added value and a sense of belonging.

☐ **ART #94:** Consider innovative sponsorship partnerships that deliver more value-added benefits for your customers, such as Amazon's partnership with publishers for certain online reading groups.

☐ **ART #95:** Look for opportunities to partner with, communicate with, and promote independent user groups of your product or service.

☐ **ART #96:** Monitor negative reviews in user groups and through social media channels like Twitter for potential service problems that you can rectify.

☐ **ART #97:** Don't try to remove negative comments about your company from discussion groups, social media channels, and other points of contact with your community. Hearing about the good, the bad, and the ugly will help you do a better job of serving your very best customers.

☐ **ART #98:** Your involvement in charities (local and/or global) can enhance your customers' perceptions of your organization.

☐ **ART #99:** Promote your organization's charitable causes using the same themes you use to promote your brand in the for-profit realm.

☐ **ART #100:** You can create an even stronger relationship with your best customers by inspiring them to partner with you in your charitable efforts.

AMAZEMENT REVOLUTION TAKEAWAYS: WALK THE WALK

☐ **ART #101:** Identify core committable values—values that you will hire for or fire for—that support your organization's service mission.

☐ **ART #102:** Make passion for service a core committable value.

☐ **ART #103:** Transparency and open communication are important core committable values that can support customer-focused organizations when modeled from the top down.

☐ **ART #104**: Make sure management and senior executives have direct, regular, face-to-face exposure to the customer service environment, and that they consistently model the same behaviors and meet the same standards they expect from front-line employees.

☐ **ART #105**: Senior management must not expect employees to do anything they themselves haven't done and are ready to do again if necessary. For example, if the CEO is not willing to take a call from a customer on the toll-free line, there's a problem.

☐ **ART #106**: "All for one and one for all" customer service is everyone's job. Service is not a department. It's a philosophy!

☐ **ART #107**: If you expect your employees to go the extra mile for your customers, you must prove that you are willing to go the extra mile for them!

☐ **ART #108**: If you are a leader, you must deliver tough news in person. Don't leave the job to others.

☐ **ART #109**: An informed workforce is more confident and effective than an uninformed workforce, even when the news it has to process is difficult.

☐ **ART #110**: When you have difficult news to deliver, do it fast. Don't let rumors or paranoia set in.

☐ **ART #111**: If you are a leader, it is imperative that your personality complement your organization's mission and set the tone for all the organization's interactions with customers.

☐ **ART #112**: Walking the walk means you live and breathe your company's mission, vision, and values, and that your personality is congruent with what your company stands for.

☐ **ART #113**: Find your story. It should be one that supports your values and your organization's promise to customers. Share the story constantly; make knowing it and retelling it part of what it means to be a part of your organization.

☐ **ART #114**: Everyone must walk the walk when it comes to modeling customer service, either to external customers or internal customers (employees). This principle is extremely important because if you are not on the front line yourself, you are in a role that supports the front line, directly or indirectly!

☐ **ART #115**: Make sure everyone, at all levels, practices the Employee Golden Rule: treat your fellow employees the way you want the customer treated—maybe even better.

APPENDIX B:

AMAZEMENT BRAINSTORM
WORKSHEETS

Reading the Amazement Revolution without implementation is procrastination.

O n the following pages, you will find tools that you can use to put into action what you've learned from the book. If you were to hire one of my facilitators/trainers to conduct a customer service workshop, you would get these types of questions and exercises from them to help you start your own Amazement Revolution.

I call these exercises Amazement Brainstorms. Each one is a series of questions designed as "thought starters" to get your mind working on implementing each of the strategies in this book.

If you are working by yourself, simply reflect and make some notes in response to the questions. If you are working with a "study buddy" or in a group setting, start by working through the exercises on your own and then team up with your companions (up to four people) to compare responses and discuss your answers, thoughts, and ideas.

Take your time doing this. You can easily spend an entire day working through these worksheets. Most organizations I work with find they can benefit from spending several hours on just one of these exercises.

You'll get tremendous benefit out of these brainstorming exercises, even if you are working on your own, but if you are able to work with someone else or in a group setting, you will have an even greater advantage. There is a synergy that comes along with working with other people that allows a group to produce a result that is greater than the sum of its parts. Working by yourself, you may come up with three good ideas. Someone else working on the same question might come up with three totally different good ideas. For some reason, if you then combined your six total ideas and started talking about them, you might find that you don't have just six ideas, but several more than either of you had thought of—just as a result of engaging in the conversation. That's the principle of synergy at work. The very process of engaging in this kind of conversation is key to starting your Amazement Revolution.

Before you go any further, I encourage you to print out the workbook that is available at no charge from this book's companion Website, www.amazementrevolution.com.

Be prepared to go through the exercises more than once. Write out your thoughts, change your mind, and rewrite as you see fit.

DIRECTIONS

All of these Amazement Brainstorm exercises work the same way. First, you will choose the Amazement Strategy that you want to work on. Then you will go through what I call a thought starter. This is a series of questions that starts you thinking about how to implement the strategies. If you are working on your own, just take your time going through the questions and exercises. If you are working with another person or a group of people, note that the suggested times are *minimums*.

The following directions are for *groups of two or more people only*: Once you have completed your thought starter, you will move on to a monologue in which you will have five minutes to share your answers with the group. You will then engage in a dialogue, which is a conversation about how the ideas you've discussed might be implemented at your organization. Finally, you will report out, which means that you will share your ideas, either with other groups that may be going through the same exercise or with other people in your organization who can help you implement the great idea(s) you've come up with.

You don't have to work on all seven Amazement Strategies at once. As a matter of fact, you may choose to work on just one or two of the strategies that you consider most relevant to your particular company or to your own job responsibility. For example, if you don't hire people as part of your job, you may not want to do the brainstorm for hiring.

Your goal should be to walk away from each Amazement Brainstorm with at least one great idea to implement. If you do that, your financial investment in this book and the time you took to read and work through these exercises will be repaid exponentially!

Here's the master format:

Thought Starter (ten minutes):

- Work through the questions in the thought starters on your own.

Monologue (five minutes each):

- After writing down your answers to the thought starter, each person will have five minutes to share his or her answers. One person will do *most* of the talking (if not all) while the others listen.

Dialogue (ten minutes or more):

- After each person has shared their answers, have a conversation about how you could implement these into your organization.

Report Out (five minutes minimum per group, which includes discussion):

- If you are in a larger group setting and have broken into smaller groups of two to four people, take the time to hear the other groups' answers.
- If you are working independently or as part of a single group, report out your ideas to someone else in the organization who can implement them.

MEMBERSHIP BRAINSTORM

Thought Starter

- Think of a time you went to a private club, either as a member or guest. (If you have never been to a private club, imagine what it would be like to do so.) Make a list of answers to the following questions:
    1. What did you notice that was special?
    2. How were you treated?
    3. What did you get from a club that you wouldn't get from a typical business?
    4. What "extras" did you get that would make you want to do business or stay in contact with this organization?

Conversation

Share your answers with up to four people. Take up to five minutes for each person. Then take at least ten minutes to brainstorm how to adapt any of these ideas into your organization.

Question

If you could only implement one idea about membership, what would it be?

Report Out

If there are other groups participating in the same session, take the time for each group to share their answers and thoughts. Each group will close their presentation with their one implementable idea.

SERIOUS FUN BRAINSTORM

Thought Starter

- What are the benefits and advantages of working at your organization?
- Why would someone want to leave?
- What extra perk(s) could you offer or would you like to see offered?
- What's the one thing your employees appreciate about your organization more than anything?
- What are the reasons people choose to work here?
- What could make working for you even better?

Conversation

Share your answers with up to four people. Take up to five minutes for each person. Then take at least ten minutes to brainstorm how to bring any of these ideas into your organization.

Question

If you could only implement one FUN idea in your organization, what would it be?

Report Out

If there are other groups participating in the same session, take the time for each group to share their answers and thoughts. Each group will close their presentation with their one implementable idea.

PARTNERSHIP BRAINSTORM

Thought Starter

- Answer the question, "Why should someone do business with us instead of the competition?"
- Do any of your customers consider you a "partner"? If so, why?
- What's the biggest problem you have ever solved for a customer? This is not a complaint, but an issue or opportunity that made the customer think you were the best at what you do.
- What do you do to build confidence with your customers?

Conversation

Share your answers with up to four people. Take up to five minutes for each person. Then take at least ten minutes to brainstorm how to bring any of these ideas into your organization.

Question

If you could only implement one idea to create a partnership with your customers, what would it be?

Report Out

If there are other groups participating in the same session, take the time for each group to share their answers and thoughts. Each group will close their presentation with their one implementable idea.

HIRE RIGHT BRAINSTORM

Thought Starter

- What are your organization's core values?
- What single question could you ask a job applicant to find out whether he or she is a good fit for your organization?
- What other tactics can you use during the interview process to determine whether the applicant is a good fit for your organization's culture?
- Are you hiring for skill first or for attitude first?

Conversation

Share your answers with up to four people. Take up to five minutes for each person. Then take at least ten minutes to brainstorm how to bring any of these ideas into your organization.

Question

If you could only implement one idea about hiring, what would it be?

Report Out

If there are other groups participating in the same session, take the time for each group to share their answers and thoughts. Each group will close their presentation with their one implementable idea.

AFTER-EXPERIENCE BRAINSTORM

Thought Starter

- Think of a time you received a thank-you note or a gift of appreciation. How did it make you feel?
- What could you give your customers that would be unexpected, appreciated, and memorable? If it is a gift, what would it be? If it is a gesture or a point of contact, what would it be?

Conversation

Share your answers with up to four people. Take up to five minutes for each person. Then take at least ten minutes to brainstorm how to bring any of these ideas into your organization.

Question

If you could only implement one idea about the after-experience, what would it be?

Report Out

If there are other groups participating in the same session, take the time for each group to share their answers and thoughts. Each group will close their presentation with their one implementable idea.

COMMUNITY BRAINSTORM

Thought Starter

- Are you part of a user group or forum outside your workplace? If so, what do you get out of being a part of that group? (If you haven't participated in such a group, just go on to the next question.)
- What could you do to bring your customers together in such a group?
- What forum could you create to get better customer feedback and more ideas for improvement?
- If a customer has a suggestion, do you have a system in place to give the idea consideration—or even implementation?
- What forum could you create to get feedback that is specific to the product or service you sell? This is not about customer service, but the actual product or service delivered. (See the Harley-Davidson example on page 137.)

Conversation

Share your answers with up to four people. Take up to five minutes for each person. Then take at least ten minutes to brainstorm how to bring any of these ideas into your organization.

Question

If you could only implement one idea about building a community, what would it be?

Report Out

If there are other groups participating in the same session, take the time for each group to share their answers and thoughts. Each group will close their presentation with their one implementable idea.

WALK THE WALK BRAINSTORM

This is a much bigger topic than the other six Amazement Brainstorms. You could potentially spend hours—or even days—answering the following questions about how your organization can walk the walk.

Thought Starter (twenty minutes minimum)

- What do you stand for as an individual?
- What does your organization stand for?
- How do your values and your personality match up with your organization's?
- What are your organization's core committable values? (Core committable values are values you would hire and fire for. See the Zappos example on page 155.)
- On a scale of one to ten, with ten being best, how well would you say you are in alignment with those values? How well would you say your organization as a whole is in alignment with those values?

Conversation

Share your answers with up to four people. Take up to five minutes for each person. Now take at least ten minutes to brainstorm how to bring any of these ideas into your organization.

Question

If you could only implement one idea to walk the walk, what would it be?

Report Out

If there are other groups participating in the same session, take the time for each group to share their answers and thoughts. Each group will close their presentation with their one implementable idea.

NOTES

CHAPTER 2: HOW WE GOT HERE

1. Shep Hyken, *The Cult of the Customer* (New York: John Wiley & Sons, 2009).
2. Jan Carlzon, *Moments of Truth* (New York: Harper Paperbacks, 1989).
3. "American Express Wins Customer Service Award, Unveils New Study," *e-commerceINSIGHTS.com*, http://www.ecommerceinsights. com, July 2010.

CHAPTER 3: THE MASTER CLASS

1. Interviews with Jim Bush, August 2010.
2. The Cooper Collection of American Transportation History, reproduction of American Express Co. shipping receipt, New York, August 6, 1853.

3. "I Love American Express," http://www.fink-think.blogspot.com.

4. "J.D. Power 2010 Credit Card Satisfaction Survey–Guess Who's #1?" *Doughroller*, August 19, 2010, http://www.doughroller.net.

CHAPTER 4: PROVIDE MEMBERSHIP

1. "The Power of Personal Service," http://www.jobs.fourseasons.com.

2. Better Business Bureau, "Vision, Mission and Values," http://www.bbb.org.

3. Better Business Bureau, "Standards for Trust," http://www.bbb.org.

4. Northern Lights Credit Union, http://www.nlcu.on.ca.

5. Entrepreneurs' Organization, http://www.eonetwork.org.

6. Entrepreneurs' Organization, http://www.eonetwork.org.

CHAPTER 5: SERIOUS FUN

1. "CDC Recognizes Baptist Health for Obesity Programs," *Coral Gables Gazette*, July 30, 2009.

2. "Critical Care," *Smart Business (Miami)*, December 2005.

3. "Are People Your Priority?" *Healthcare Executive*, July/August 2004.

4. "Critical Care," *Smart Business (Miami)*, December 2005.

5. Baptist Health South Florida, http://www.baptisthealth.net.

6. The Robert Wood Johnson Foundation, "Nurse Residency Programs Emerging as Popular Retention Tactic," http://www.rwjf.org.

7. Baptist Health South Florida, http://www.baptisthealth.net.

8. StuderGroup, http://www.studergroup.com.

9. "Critical Care," *Smart Business (Miami)*, December 2005.

10. Ceridian, "Customer Spotlight: Ceridian Helps Alston & Bird Raise the Bar with Self-service Solutions," http://www.ceridian.com.

11. "How to Ensure Lateral Loyalty," *American Lawyer*, November 20, 2007.

12. "The Google Way: Give Engineers Room," *New York Times*, October 21, 2007.

13. Slalom Consulting, http://www.slalom.com.
14. Marketwire, "Slalom Consulting Named One of Chicago's Best and Brightest Companies to Work For," June 2009.
15. Interview with Tom Klobucher, October 2010.
16. SAS, http://blogs.sas.com.
17. The Scooter Store, "The SCOOTER Store Named One of Fortune's 100 Best Companies to Work For in 2010," http://media.thescooterstore.com.

CHAPTER 6: CULTIVATE PARTNERSHIP

1. Interview with Matthew Porter.
2. Yelp, http://www.yelp.com.
3. Quick Transportation, http://www.quicktransportation.com.

CHAPTER 7: HIRE RIGHT

1. The Fudgery, http://www.fudgeryfudge.com.
2. New Chapter, http://www.newchapter.com.
3. Robert Spector, *The Nordstrom Way to Customer Service Excellence: A Handbook For Implementing Great Service in Your Organization* (New York: John Wiley & Sons, 2005).
4. "Consumer Reports Ranks Top Supermarkets," http://www.cleveland.com, April 6, 2009.
5. "Finding Workers Who Fit: The Container Store Built a Booming Business for Neatniks—Who Turned Out to Be Their Best Employees," *Business 2.0*, November 2004.
6. Hy-Vee, http://www.hy-vee.com.
7. *The (Un)Secret Shopper*, http://www.theunsecretshopper.com.
8. Insider Pages, http://www.insiderpages.com.
9. Yelp, http://www.yelp.com.

CHAPTER 8:

1. Ranoush, http://www.ranoush.com.

CHAPTER 9: BUILD COMMUNITY

1. Insider Pages, http://www.insiderpages.com.
2. "In-N-Out Burger vs. McDonald's: Guess Who Won?" *Wall Street Journal*, January 28, 2009.
3. *GoodFinancialCents*, http://www.goodfinancialcents.com.
4. Apple User Groups, http://www.apple.com/usergroups.

CHAPTER 10: WALK THE WALK

1. Evan Carmichael, http://www.evancarmichael.com.
2. Zappos, http://www.zappos.com.
3. Tony Hsieh, interview by Tavis Smiley, *Tavis Smiley*, June 30, 2010.
4. Tony Hsieh, *Delivering Happiness: A Path to Profits, Passion, and Purpose* (New York: Business Plus, 2010).
5. Michael Eisner, *Work in Progress: Risking Failure, Surviving Success* (New York: Hyperion, 1999).
6. L.L. Bean, http://www.llbean.com.
7. "Flying High with Herb Kelleher: A Profile in Charismatic Leadership," *Journal of Leadership Studies*, June 22, 1999.

ACKNOWLEDGMENTS

F irst, I want to thank you, the reader, for investing in this book. I hope you get a tremendous amount of value for the time you take to read it and work through the exercises in appendix B. My philosophy about any book on business is to learn and implement just one idea; anything more is a bonus. This book is filled with ideas, and I hope you find so many that you have a difficult time choosing which one you will implement first.

A special thank you for all of the great clients I get to work with. Every time I work with any of you I learn something new, which is how I develop new material. In addition, many of you have discussed the strategies covered in this book over the last several years. Your feedback and comments have helped me formulate and fine-tune the content of this book.

Thank you to Brandon Toropov for his hard work. More than an editor, he has been my sounding board and offered many ideas on how to make the book better.

Thank you to Lauren Manoy who did the final rounds of editing. I'd like to blame any mistakes that you find on her, but I won't. I'll take full responsibility for any typos or misspellings you might find. With that said, I love what Mark Twain once said: "I feel bad for the man that can't spell a word more than one way."

Thank you to Jerry Dorris at AuthorSupport for the interior design of the book. Jerry has great creativity and gives amazing customer service.

Thank you to my friends at Greenleaf Book Group. The team at GBK gave me a tremendous amount of support and help in bringing this book from a manuscript to the book you now have in your hands.

Finally, thank you to my family, which includes my wife, Cindy; my son, Brian; and my daughters, Alex and Casey. When my clients hire me to consult or speak at their meetings, they have no idea that they are pulling me away from a wonderful family who accepts that I'm not home every night for dinner. And, even when I was home, there were quite a few evenings that I retreated to work on the book. I appreciate their love, support, patience, and enthusiasm for this project.

INDEX

BY SUBJECT

INDEX

BY COMPANY

ABOUT THE AUTHOR

SHEP HYKEN, CSP, CPAE, is the Chief Amazement Officer of Shepard Presentations. As a speaker and author, Shep works with companies and organizations who want to build loyal relationships with their customers and employees. His articles have been read in hundreds of publications, and he is the author of *Moments of Magic*, *The Loyal Customer* and the *Wall Street Journal* and *USA Today* best seller *The Cult of the Customer*. He is also the creator of the Customer Focus™ program, which helps clients develop a customer service culture and loyalty mindset.

In 1983 Shep founded Shepard Presentations and since then has worked with hundreds of clients ranging from Fortune 100 organizations to companies with less than fifty employees. Some of his clients include American Airlines, AAA, Anheuser-Busch, AT&T, AETNA, Abbott Laboratories, American Express—and that's just a few of the A's!

Shep Hyken's most requested programs focus on customer service, customer loyalty, internal service, customer relations, and the customer experience. He is known for his high-energy presentations, which combine important information with entertainment (humor and magic) to create exciting programs for his audiences.

(CPAE, or the Council of Peers Award for Excellence, is the National Speakers Association's Speaker Hall of Fame award for lifetime achievement in the area platform/speaking excellence. CSP is the international designation for Certified Speaking Professionals and is awarded to individuals for certain achievements and education in the speaking profession.)

Contact Shepard Presentations for more information on Shep Hyken's speaking and customer service training programs as well as his books and other knowledge products.

Shepard Presentations, LLC
(314) 692-2200
E-mail: shep@hyken.com — Web: http://www.hyken.com